How Does God Speak?

The Three-Dimensional Ways

By

Jeremy Lopez

How Does God Speak? The Three-
Dimensional Ways

By Dr. Jeremy Lopez

Copyright © 2019

Published by Identity Network

P.O. Box 383213 Birmingham, AL 35238

www.IdentityNetwork.net

ENDORSEMENTS

"You are put on this earth with incredible potential and a divine destiny. This powerful, practical man shows you how to tap into powers you didn't even know you had." – Brian Tracy – Author, *The Power of Self Confidence*

"I found myself savoring the concepts of the Law of Attraction merging with the Law of Creativity until slowly the beautiful truths seeped deeper into my thirsty soul. I am called to be a Creator! My friend, Dr. Jeremy Lopez, has a way of reminding us of our eternal 'I-Am-ness' while putting the tools in our hands to unlock our endless creative potential with the Divine mind. As a musical composer, I'm

excited to explore, with greater understanding, the infinite realm of possibilities as I place fingers on my piano and whisper, 'Let there be!'" – Dony McGuire, Grammy Award winning artist and musical composer

"Jeremy dives deep into the power of consciousness and shows us that we can create a world where the champion within us can shine and how we can manifest our desires to live a life of fulfillment. A must read!" – Greg S. Reid – Forbes and Inc. top rated Keynote Speaker

"I have been privileged to know Jeremy Lopez for many years, as well as sharing the platform with him at a number of conferences. Through this time, I have found him as a man of integrity, commitment, wisdom, and one of the most networked people I have met. Jeremy is an

entrepreneur and a leader of leaders. He has amazing insights into leadership competencies and values. He has a passion to ignite this latent potential within individuals and organizations and provide ongoing development and coaching to bring about competitive advantage and success. I would recommend him as a speaker, coach, mentor, and consultant." – Chris Gaborit – Learning Leader, Training & Outsourcing Entrepreneur

ACKNOWLEDGMENTS

To all who, like me, have a desire to hear the voice of God, I offer this book to you. My prayer is that you would experience the voice of God in all areas of your life and that you would know His Presence more intimately than ever before.

CONTENTS

INTRODUCTION

How does God speak? "God works in mysterious ways," we've so often heard. It's true. The same could be said, though, of the ways in which God speaks. It's in the stillness and in the quiet that we hear the voice of God, yes. And it's also in the thunder and in the lightning and in raging winds. What I began to realize within my own life those years ago when I found myself consumed with the prophetic gift, inspired to take the Gospel to the ends of the earth through what would come to be the global outreach of Identity Network, I realized that God is always speaking. Not even once has there ever been a moment in which humanity has been without the voice of the Holy Spirit – even when the voice has gone unnoticed and unrecognized. For decades, I've been led to share with the world the power of the prophetic, and through countless millions of prophetic words delivered what I've come to realize all the more is that the voice of the Holy Spirit is always in operation.

I felt the leading of the Holy Spirit to write this book because it seems that so often, when speaking of the subject of the voice of God, the concept can be such a misnomer. How often has it been said when catastrophe comes or when productivity seems to be nonexistent that someone has "missed God?" You're, I'm sure, familiar with the idea. When something seems to go off the rails and when the unexpected moments of life arise, so many have been conditioned by religion to believe, rather erroneously, that the trials have come only because they've "missed God." As I shared within my book *What Doesn't Kill You Makes You Stronger*, though, such is simply not the case – nor has it ever been. Today as never before the Body of Christ and, yes, the entire world at large has such a rudimentary and elementary understanding of the voice of God that all too often individuals seem to miss the forest for the trees, as the old saying goes.

What if what you've been seeking has truly been seeking after you the entire time? What if there has never been a moment of your life in which the voice of the Holy Spirit has not been present? Furthermore, what if it can be shown – proven, even – that humanity, at its most basic nature, has been created to hear the voice of God? Would such a revelation not only change the way that we view humanity but also, even more importantly, serve to change the way in which we view God? It simply cannot be stressed enough, though, and it must be stressed here at the very offset that the time has come for the Body of Christ to grow up in its understanding of God's voice. The time has come to put away childish things and to, as Paul declared, have the eyes of our understanding enlightened. As we journey together through the pages of this book, you will begin to understanding that the voice of God has always been much larger, much broader, and even more expansive – more powerful – than the religions of the world have ever dared to admit.

The Holy Scriptures serve to illustrate for us the effects – the impact – of the voice of God, detailing how lives were transformed and changed as the Word of God came to men and women just like us. In fact, today, there would not be a Holy Bible as we now know it without the voice of the Holy Spirit and without mankind's ability to hear God clearly. But what if the voice of God, like the Presence of God, is actually much, much more universal a concept than we have ever dared to think or to imagine? What if the voice of God, contrary to the teachings of religion, is actually much more innate, more latent within all of humanity and not confined solely to cathedrals or to pulpits or to the traveling evangelists – or even to prophets, for that matter? Although I consider it such a tremendous honor to deliver the Word of the LORD to individuals from all walks of life, I consider it such a highlight of my life and my work in ministry when individuals, just like you, learn to hear the voice of God for themselves.

Yes, the word of the LORD can and should always be confirmed. And, yes, the LORD still speaks through the gift of the prophetic and the prophetic voice has never ceased within the realm of earth. However, there is something truly heavenly that begins to happen when individuals begin to hear the voice of the LORD for themselves, within their own personal lives. Something truly remarkable begins to happen when, from the least to the greatest, the revelation of the voice of God begins to become fully alive within the hearts and the minds of men and women. Did you know that you, too, possess the ability to prophesy and to call things into existence? Did you know that the same prophetic voice which has shaken nations and crumbled empires throughout history is the exact same voice now dwelling within you even as you read these words? It's true.

To better begin to understand the role the voice of the Holy Spirit plays within the hearts and the minds of men and women, though, requires a better understanding of the prophetic gift. Can all prophesy? Can all feel the inspiration of the LORD within them and, most importantly, interpret that inner voice correctly? According to religious tradition, the role of the prophetic voice has been relegated only to a select few – to seers and to mystics or to those who hold the "office" of the prophet. However, if we were to delve more deeply into the sacred text of the Holy Scriptures and also were to begin to discover the rich history of the early church in Jerusalem following the glorious outpouring at Pentecost, we would find that the "gift" of prophecy has always, always existed within humanity – even before the worlds were ever formed.

What I find day by day and continue to see all the more is that men and women across the globe, regardless of their faith or religious tradition, not only have a desire to hear the voice of God for themselves but, above all, they desire to hear the voice of God clearly, accurately, and unmistakably for themselves. Yes, the role of the office of the prophet is needed and is just as important as it ever was; however, there is something truly remarkable that begins to happen when the prophetic gift is awakened within a seeker in a very personal way – in a very private, inner way. Suddenly, things begin to change as the atmosphere of uncertainty begins to shift and become transformed into a reality of absolute certainty and knowing. All of the sudden, as the voice of God is heard clearly – accurately – the feeling of uncertainty gives way to a boldness that can only come from a sense of absolute certainty. You can possess this certainty. In fact, as you will soon realize and discover as you journey with me through the pages of this book, you already do possess it, in fact. You possess it even when you do not feel it and even when it may not seem like it.

It's time to move into a realm of greater certainty and an even greater assurance – an assurance that transcends mere thought and mere believing. I've often said that, in reality, "belief" is just another term for "insecurity." Think of it. When you say, "I believe," what you're in fact saying is, "I think, but I don't really *know*." With every belief comes a sense of uncertainty. Belief, in and of itself, can sometimes be considered nothing more than a guessing game – a game in which the mind struggles to grasp hold of something that makes sense, without ever fully having a concrete, evidential foundation to stand upon. If you are ever going to allow the prophetic gift to awaken within you and if you are ever going to hear the voice of God clearly, for yourself, you're going to have to move from the place of mere believing to the place of pure knowing. It's not enough for you to simply believe that you hear from God. It's time that you know it, without question. It's time to settle the issue once and for all and to put to rest the age-old question, "Does God still speak?"

Today, as you read these words, my prayer for you is that you would allow your faith to move beyond the realm of wishful thinking and hoping to a place of absolute knowing. It's within the knowing – within the absolute certainty – that the realm of Heaven is revealed all the more. Honestly, contrary to the lies of religion, it's really not enough to simply believe blindly, without question. The church was built upon knowing and not upon thinking, wishing, and guessing. In order to make the gift of faith more of a firm foundation – a foundation capable of settling all doubt and unbelief – there must first come a shift from uncertainty to absolute knowing. And when the knowing comes, never again will you ever feel the need to seek after the voice of God outside or apart from yourself. Can you imagine what life would be like if you could *know* that you're hearing the voice of God clearly for yourself?

What happens within the life of a believer when they begin to move into the realm of knowing, rather than the place of hoping, wishing, and guessing? A confidence comes. An assurance comes. Doubt gives way to belief, and, as Jesus said, all things are possible to those who believe. In his teachings during his earthly life and ministry, Jesus continually taught that we would be given exactly what we believe. Yet, how often have we created only more doubt and unbelief for ourselves simply because we weren't entirely sure that we had heard the voice of God clearly? Simply because we weren't sure that we had felt the inspiration of the Holy Spirit within our lives? Simply because we operated from the realm of "I think" rather than from the realm of "I know?" Yes, there is much to be said about the realm of knowing – the place of blessed assurance and confidence. And that is why I am sharing this revelation with you, my fellow believer and seeker.

"Cease not to give thanks for you, making mention of you in my prayers; That the God of our Lord Jesus Christ, the Father of glory, may give unto you the spirit of wisdom and revelation in the knowledge of him: The eyes of your understanding being enlightened; that ye may know what is the hope of his calling, and what the riches of the glory of his inheritance in the saints, And what is the exceeding greatness of his power to us-ward who believe, according to the working of his mighty power, Which he wrought in Christ, when he raised him from the dead, and set him at his own right hand in the heavenly places, Far above all principality, and power, and might, and dominion, and every name that is named, not only in this world, but also in that which is to come: And hath put all

things under his feet, and gave him to be the head over all things to the church, Which is his body, the fulness of him that filleth all in all." (Ephesians 1:16-23 KJV) Within Paul's epistle to the church at Ephesus, he equates the hope of the calling to a sense of knowing, stating that when the eyes of our understanding become enlightened we will *know* the hope of our calling. To move from the realm of knowing from the place of mere thinking or wishing requires a certain sense of understanding – a sense of awakened enlightenment.

It's time to know the truth, once and for all. It's time to finally put to rest the age-old question "Does God still speak?" It's time to understand the truth, once and for all, that not only does God still speak continuously but that you have within your own genetic makeup the power and the ability to hear the voice of God clearly. It's time to know, as never before, that you have been designed, by intelligent, loving design, to not only have communion and fellowship with the Creator but that you've been designed to hear with precision and clarity every single word that proceeds out of the mouth of God. It's not enough, you see, to simply hear from God; it's imperative – expedient – that you hear with greater precision and clarity. It's time to know the voice of God within your own life.

You've been given many great and wonderful promises – promises that demand your attention if you are to ever lay hold to all that waits for you. You and I, by divine design and by Heavenly mandate, are in relationship at all times with the Divine and are daily given the opportunity to experience the realm of Heaven. Could you imagine, though, what a relationship would be like if communication didn't exist – or if communication as merely one-sided? Would there be a sense of closeness in a relationship such as that? Would there be a sense of intimacy? Of course not. However, within the Body of Christ, for far too long there has been only the existence of one-sided conversation. Many believe that God speaks yet never truly hear the voice within with precision and clarity. Others speak without ever really taking the time to listen and to understand. For centuries, in fact, religion has served only to numb the senses – only to anesthetize the hearts and the minds of men and women, keeping them in a place of questioning and uncertainty. Religion is deadly.

As I've said for years and have seen confirmed all the more within my own life and ministry, prayer is not a religious guessing game. It is not mere wishful thinking. Prayer is a state of being; it is a perpetual state of existence. It is an existence founded upon the sense of knowing and not a mere believing or hoping or guessing. When knowing comes, even the way that one views the concept of prayer begins to change. Prayer becomes much more than some religious act and, instead, becomes a state of perpetual bliss – a journey of discovery rather than some mere act of speaking or hearing. I refuse to ever believe that faith is simple guessing, hoping, or wishing because the scriptures in no way teach that. As we delve into the scriptures, we find that the church was built upon the bedrock of absolute assurance – a concrete state of constant knowing. Even Jesus himself stated as much, when he spoke of the Holy Spirit that would baptize believers.

"These things have I spoken unto you, that ye should not be offended. They shall put you out of the synagogues: yea, the time cometh, that whosoever killeth you will think that he doeth God service. And these things will they do unto you, because they have not known the Father, nor me. But these things have I told you, that

when the time shall come, ye may remember that I told you of them. And these things I said not unto you at the beginning, because I was with you. But now I go my way to him that sent me; and none of you asketh me, Whither goest thou? But because I have said these things unto you, sorrow hath filled your heart. Nevertheless I tell you the truth; It is expedient for you that I go away: for if I go not away, the Comforter will not come unto you; but if I depart, I will send him unto you. And when he is come, he will reprove the world of sin, and of righteousness, and of judgment: Of sin, because they believe not on me; Of righteousness, because I go to my Father, and ye see me no more; Of judgment, because the prince of this world is judged. I have yet many things to say unto you, but ye cannot bear them now. Howbeit when he, the Spirit of truth, is come, he will guide you into all truth: for he shall not speak of himself; but whatsoever he shall hear, that shall he speak: and he will shew you things to come. He shall glorify me: for he shall receive of mine, and shall shew it unto you." *(John 16:1-14 KJV)*

Notice that when Jesus spoke of the Holy Spirit who would come to empower and to embolden believers, he spoke of the importance of knowing, stating that we would be led into all truth – not some truth and not partial truth. Selective, partial truth by definition is not truth. Partial truth is not all truth. You and I have been given a promise – an assurance and a blessed hope. We have been promised that we will be led into all truth. Truth, though, doesn't always come easily. It isn't something is magically, spiritually imparted or suddenly dropped into our laps from above. Truth must be discovered. It must be recognized. And when it is recognized, it can be known.

Communication with Heaven is the key to this knowing.

CHAPTER ONE

BEYOND RELIGION

It was Evagrius Ponticus, in his work *The Praktikos*, who said, "Prayer is an ascent of the spirit to God." And it was Brother Lawrence, in his dissertation entitled *The Practice of the Presence of* God, who said, simply, "God has many ways of drawing us to Himself." For most of my life, for as long as I can remember even, I've been a student of the sacred scriptures, feeling within me for as long as I can even recall a desire to study the scriptures in the light of truth, particularly where the voice of God is concerned. When I began to become aware all those years ago of my own prophetic gift, recognizing that I was being called to take the prophetic voice to the uttermost parts of the world, I found myself questioning all the more the mechanics and the dynamics of the voice of the LORD. For me, it was never enough to simply know that God speaks. I was determined to better understand exactly how and why God speaks. What are the mechanics? How does the voice of the LORD come to humanity? Most importantly of all, how do we correctly hear and interpret the voice when it comes to us?

To better understand the concept of prayer, as it relates to hearing the voice of God, it is vitally important that we have a better understanding of prophecy – understanding more just exactly *how* God speaks. Is prayer, as some suggest, simply a religious ritual? Is prayer an act that takes place in moments of need? Or is prayer, rather, something much greater? Is prayer something much more? To even begin to better understand how one hears and interprets the voice of God is to, first, recognize the power of belief and to gain a more comprehensive understanding of the role faith plays in all of our prayers and also in our ability to hear and to discern. How often has it seemed that you've "missed it" where the voice of God is concerned? How often has it felt as though the heavens were made brass and that your prayers never were heard? Furthermore, how many times has it seemed that God never seemed to be speaking – often when you needed His voice most? In order to move to a greater realm of assurance where the voice of God is concerned demands that we begin with honesty. The brutal honesty is that for so long we've viewed the concept of hearing God in all the wrong ways because of religion and because of faulty, erroneous doctrine concerning prayer and the prophetic voice.

When I felt the inspiration of the Holy Spirit to write what would become what is, to date, one of my bestselling books *Prayer: Think Without Ceasing*, I felt such an overwhelming presence of the LORD regarding the revelation that came to me. In the book, I stressed the importance of moving from the place of believing to the realm of knowing – a shift that, at least according to the Apostles, is needed if we are ever to come into a greater measure of the miraculous. As I began to study the sacred text of the Holy Scriptures, what began to become immediately clear to me is that the early church did not view the voice of prayer the way that the modern, more religious church of today does. In fact, even prior to the birth of Christendom, even prior to Pentecost at Jerusalem, the scriptures bear out that all throughout history men and women have possessed the ability to not only hear the voice of God but also to hear it clearly – to hear it precisely and without fail. Clarity, it seems, was always crucial in every moment of communion with God.

Even in the very Beginning, we find the element of communion, as the Creator came to the Garden to walk with His Creation in the cool of the day. Imagine that for a moment. Even in the Beginning, we find that Heaven wanted to communicate! Long before there was ever a man and a woman and even before the worlds were ever even formed and before the stars were first hurled onto the tapestry of the night sky, there was the theme of communication. In the very Beginning, "God said." To even delve into the great, rich history of the faith is to have a need to better understand communication, in that the very scriptures which serve as the basis of the faith begin with the topic. According to the faith, words were being spoken long, long before the Earth ever existed. We then find that, even before man was ever formed and fashioned from the dust of the ground, the Creator said, "Let us make man in our image." Here at the very offset into our journey into a better understanding of the voice of God, I would ask, just who, exactly, was He speaking to? Was He simply speaking to Himself? Was He merely speaking out loud in some attempt to hear Himself speak, wondering if His ideas were somehow, someway valid or warranted? Surely not.

What if I were to tell you that the Creator, even then, was speaking directly to you? What if I were to tell you that even then, long before the worlds were ever formed, the Creator desired communication with you? Would such a claim seem outlandish or unbelievable? You may ask, "Jeremy, how can this even be?" Though such a claim may seem shocking to the religious, natural mind, the Holy Scriptures bear out that long before anything else – or anyone else –

existed, even then there existed the voice of God and the desire within the heart of God to communicate. Long before you were ever formed and fashioned within your mother's womb, you possessed an uncanny knack for communicating with God. The Prophet Jeremiah declares that even before you were ever formed within your mother's womb, you were *known* by God. Such a shocking claim seems to fly in the face of religious orthodoxy which, for generations, has sought to claim that prayer and communication with God are simply aspects of religious practice.

What if I were to even suggest to you that you've always been communicating with God even when you didn't realize it? That you, in fact, could not even cease from communicating with God even if you were ever to try? Would such a claim not only change the way that you view prayer but also serve to enlighten the eyes of your understanding so that you could better understand the truth regarding communion with the Divine? I ask these questions because, in truth, it was this perspective which dominated the early church and accounted for the many moments of miraculous intervention – those moments in which Heaven seemed to so often, so naturally invade the realm of Earth. As you study the sacred text of the Holy Scriptures, you will find that the realm of Heaven never once seemed some distant or far-off place. Heaven, rather, in often the most shocking and most unbelievable of ways seemed to be a mere extension of natural, daily life. If you've never taken the time to think of it from this perspective, simply read the Book of Acts. The realm of Heaven was such a natural, everyday extension of normal life upon Planet Earth that, for the Apostles, angelic help was the norm, miracles occurred daily, and the Gospel of the Kingdom was taken to the uttermost parts of the known world. Suffice it to say, then, there was a sense of knowing – a sense of absolute certainty that seemed to far surpass and even supersede the simple, shallow, "childlike" faith of today's religious creeds.

Today, though, we seem to settle for far, far less. "Just believe," we're so often told. "Just believe that you're hearing from God. Step out on faith." With this lack of certainty, though, comes a lack of evidence. I've often said for years that faith, at least according to the scriptures, is not some force that must be trusted blindly. Faith, in fact, is never blind. It can be seen while in the land of the living. It can be proven, according to the Book of James. Above all, it can be evidenced. The issue is not simply a matter of belief but more so a matter of evidential experience. Did you know that it's not only possible to hear the voice of God and know that God is speaking but that it is also possible to actually experience the voice of God for yourself? It's true.

This journey into the deeper, greater, more transcendent revelation of the voice of God begins with a better understanding that God has always been speaking, even before the Beginning, and that there has never been a time in which God has ever really been silent. Even in the very Beginning, there existed the Word and the ability to speak and to communicate. We find this truth illustrated in the synoptic Gospel of John. Unlike the other Gospels, the writer of John seems to share the voice of God in such a cryptic, somewhat even mystical way by announcing that in the very Beginning the Word existed and that all things came from the Word - meaning that all existence within Creation has come from God's ability to speak and to utter words. Language and the ability to communicate not only formed the worlds but also inspired the creation of mankind, for it was with God's very own breath that man became a living, breathing soul.

"In the beginning was the Word, and the Word was with God, and the Word was God. The same was in the beginning with God. All things were made by him; and without him was not any thing made that was made. In him was life; and the life was the light of men. And the light shineth in darkness; and the darkness comprehended it not. There was a man sent from God, whose name was John. The same came for a witness, to bear witness of the Light, that all men through him might believe. He was not that Light, but was sent to bear witness of that Light. That was the true Light, which lighteth every man that cometh into the world. He was in the world, and the world was made by him, and the world knew him not. He came unto his own, and his own received him not. But

as many as received him, to them gave he power to become the sons of God, even to them that believe on his name: Which were born, not of blood, nor of the will of the flesh, nor of the will of man, but of God. And the Word was made flesh, and dwelt among us, (and we beheld his glory, the glory as of the only begotten of the Father,) full of grace and truth." (John 1:1-14 KJV)

In this emphatic declaration, the writer of the Gospel of John seems to suggest that all Creation itself is based entirely upon communication with God – and upon man's ability to remember that God is always speaking. All things that we see, according to the text, has come from the Creator's ability to speak – from the Word. And within these statements we find something even more remarkable: Communication from God and also with God existed before anything else. The passage also seems to depict a certain sense of human forgetfulness – a forgetfulness seemingly ingrained within the human condition. The writer seems to suggest, in some way, mankind had forgotten that it could actually hear from God. Mankind, in some way, had forgotten that it possessed the ability to communicate with God. Though the worlds were made by the Word, the world didn't recognize the Word. "The world knew Him not," according to the text.

Here at the very offset of our journey together, I want to encourage you to become open to looking beyond that you currently believe regarding prayer, prophecy, and communion with God. In order for the mind to be renewed and transformed, the mind must first be stretched. It must be pulled. It's time to begin to consider the voice of God in a much more all-encompassing way – not merely as some religious ritual or practice. Never once have you been apart from or separated from the voice of God. And, as you will see, the voice of God has always been a very present, very real reality within your life all along. Yes, the Word of the LORD can be confirmed through the gift of prophecy in others; however, what the Holy Spirit wants you to begin to discover within your own life is that the prophetic voice has always existed within you, personally – individually. Though the prophetic voice serves a very real, very important role in the collective – the ecclesia – of believers, the prophetic voice serves an even greater, more personal role within the daily life of the seeker. It's time to begin to consider just how immense, how very vast and transcendent the voice of God truly is.

What if God speaks not only in the still small voice but also in the thunder and in the lightning? What if the voice of the LORD has been equally as present in the storms as in the calmness and in the bliss of your moments of triumph? Allow me to say it another way – in an even more practical way. What if the voice of God was leading you even in the midst of your divorce? What if the voice of the Holy Spirit was leading you through your search for a more meaningful career, after the loss of your job? In fact, what if it was actually the voice of the LORD leading you to something new, something more refreshing, more satisfying the entire time anyway? You see, when we consider the immense gravity of the voice of God within our lives, we cannot afford to do so in a programmed and religious way. The voice of God is far too immense and far too transcendent to be confined to religious ritual and dogmatic creeds. The voice of God cannot be relegated to man-made rules and regulations.

Religion has always been the enemy of the moving of the Holy Spirit. In fact, the natural, religious mind – the "carnal mind" – has always been the very "enemy" of God, according to the text of the Holy Scriptures. For the mind to be renewed, the old paradigms of limitation must first be confronted and challenged. Old idols which we've erected within our minds must be torn down and destroyed in order for the truth of the voice of God to become more recognized. Today, I want you, here at the very offset of our journey together, to begin to view the voice of God in a more transcendent, more expansive way. I want to encourage you to begin to recognize that the voice of God has been leading you all along. The first step in recognizing the voice of God is to begin to settle within your mind once and for all that not only *can* you hear God but that you, in fact *do*.

Something truly remarkable – truly heavenly – begins to happen when a seeker comes to the place of knowing, moving from the realm of doubt and mere guessing toward the place of greater, blessed assurance. In order to hear the voice of God more clearly, more accurately and more precisely, you're going to have to come to the place of understanding that, although it may not always feel like it, yes you *can* and yes you *do*. Settle it within you remind once and for all that not only does God desire to speak to you but that God, in His love and mercy, has always been leading you the entire time. As the great Christian mystics wrote and taught, you are continuously being led into the Spirit. And, yes, contrary to popular belief and religious notion, God has many, many unique and different ways of drawing us to Himself. Yes, the voice of God is still in existence within the quiet place of the still, small voice; however, the voice of God has always been in existence, too, in the raging

storms, in the thunder, and in the lightning –
sometimes even literally, as you will soon see!

All of Creation, including your very own human
body, has been designed in such a way as to
promote continuous communication with the
realms of Heaven. You've been called to bring
the realm of Heaven to Earth; yes. But what if
you could begin to see that the realm of Heaven
has always, always existed within the realm of
Earth the entire time? Within the hearts of men
and women? What if you could begin to see as
never before that by design and by love,
everything in existence is continually,
constantly attempting to remind you of the voice
of God in existence? Not only would such a
revelation serve to transform your prayer life
but it would also serve to shake you from the
complacency that comes from religious notions.
Such a revelation, such an understanding, would
serve to move you toward the place of knowing.

After all, it is in the place of knowing – not guessing – that clarity, accuracy, and precision come all the more.

CHAPTER TWO

THAT YOU MIGHT KNOW

When I began to realize years ago that faith is much more than some mere guessing game or some game of chance, it began to become increasingly more clear to me that the voice of God has always been a present, very real reality – even within the realm of Earth. All of Creation, at some deep, inner level, seems to know innately, instinctively, that God desires relationship; however, all too often, we never fully take the time to awaken to what such a concept might truly mean. To even begin to come close to understanding the covenantal relationship that we have with the Creator demands that we assess and then reassess what it truly means to be in a relationship. Let's begin, first, by understanding the meaning of relationship. As you consider the term "relationship," chances are your mind begins to wander. You begin to think of the many, many wonderful people within your life.

You think of your relationships to friends, to family, and even, perhaps, to your own significant other. When we speak of "relationship," though, what we are in fact speaking of is one's ability to truly "relate." All throughout the day and night, you and I are in a constant search of relatability on some unique level. You desire greater relatability – greater understanding – in your marriage, in your career with your coworkers, and with those closest to you. In fact, even the formation of new friendships begins first, with a sense of relatability and the asking of a deep, inner question within the mind: "Can we truly relate?" At the deepest level, though, in the midst of the inner soul, lies the same desire for relatability with the Creator Himself. Deep within you exists a burning, inescapable passion and hunger to relate to the things of God. You were created in this way, and there is no escaping it. Relatability, though, in truth, can only come from proper communication – the ability to share ideas and concepts. Without communication there be no true or lasting knowledge because there can be no understanding.

In order to begin to move into a place of greater knowing and more understanding where the voice of God is concerned – in order to begin to hear and to interpret more clearly and accurately – you're going to have to realize that not only is the voice of God very present but the voice of God is also very, very relatable. It isn't distant. It isn't somehow disconnected or somehow far-off. It's very natural. It's effortless. It's just as much a part of your daily life as the very breath you breath. And like the breath you breathe, without the inner voice of God, you would not even exist.

It's high time that you begin to view the voice of God in a much more practical, much more relatable way. Remember, everything in existence operates according to very specific, very covenantal laws – the most important being "relationship." It's so easy to view the voice of God in such a spiritual, "religious" way that the voice of God begins to seem very impractical – very unnatural, even. Think of it for a moment. When someone says, "God told me," most often the mind conjures images of mystical, otherworldly experiences, often steeped in hysteria. We think of Moses being atop the mountain, seeing God in a face-to-face encounter or hearing the voice of God audibly through the flames of a burning, fiery bush. We think of prophets or visiting evangelists who declare the Word of the LORD in revival services at churches. Suffice it to say, when most think of the voice of God, they think of something very bizarre, very outrageous, and very, very, well, unrelatable.

When you begin to view the voice of God in a much more practical much more relatable and more personal way, not only will you begin to decipher the voice of communication much more clearly but you will, in turn, begin to recognize that you've never even once been without the ability to communicate with the realms of Heaven – even within your very own body, very naturally. It's time to stop relegating the voice of God simply to those voices being spoken from behind pulpits or to the voices that come only through ecstatic moments of dreams and visions. It's time to begin to access the voice of God while driving to work on your morning commute. It's time to commune with God not only before dinner but also during dinner, while you're talking to your family members and asking about their day. It's time to access the voice of God even in the midst of your disagreement with your coworkers or with your significant other. In fact, I promise you that you will be quite surprised to find the tension and the stress of the day begin to diminish when you begin to incorporate the prophetic voice into all matters of your own every day, personal life.

What if I told you that you can, at any time, get the answers you need, at any given moment of any given day and that you can have absolute assurance and absolute confidence that you've heard the voice of God clearly and accurately? You may be asking, "Well, what's the catch, Jeremy?" Well, I'm glad you asked, my friend. The "catch" is that you're going to have to change what you believe about prayer and about the voice of God and begin to start viewing the voice of God in a deeper way than ever before. In fact, the "catch" is that you're going to have to begin to actually believe that you possess the ability to communicate with God and that the voice of God is relatable and practical within your normal, everyday life. Yes, it's one thing to hear God in moments of ecstatic worship and at revivals and in moments when you're having your daily time of "prayer" and meditation; however, it's not enough. It truly isn't. When you begin to shift your perspective on prayer and prophecy, it's going to be demanded of you that you then begin to actually redefine the way that you view communication with the Holy Spirit. As I've said for years, when you change your thoughts, you change your entire life. Well, nowhere is this any truer than where the subject of hearing from God is concerned.

Personally, I used to be so uncertain. Perhaps like you, there was once a time when I questioned not only the existence of the voice of God but even more so my own ability to hear clearly and accurately. In those days, partly because of religion, I believed that the voice of God was given only during times of travail or fasting – only after I had really, really worked for it. I'm sure you've had this same belief before. Chances are you may still hold to such a belief even now. But let's be honest with ourselves for a moment. Where does such a belief truly take us? Today, there are many, many sincere and well-intentioned believers who spend days, weeks, and even months or years "praying" about whether or not God even wants them to join the choir or begin to attend a new Sunday school class. And where prayers about the new relationship or the new career are concerned, well, those can sometimes take even longer. I share these examples in all seriousness, though, to illustrate just how damaging a faulty, religious concept of prayer can truly be.

Not only is it possible to hear the voice of God clearly and accurately and without fail, it is possible to hear the voice of God quickly, at a moment's notice. Picture, if you will, a marriage relationship in which a husband or wife takes days, weeks, or even months to respond to even the most simple question? Do you truly believe that such a relationship could be lasting or even sustainable? Of course not. Even the closest of friendships begin to wane and ultimately even fall apart due to a lack of communication. Chances are, even as you read these words, you have that one "friend" who never takes the time to text you back. And chances are, even as you read these words, you probably don't place much value on that friendship the way you once did. Yet, how often have we used these very worldly, very natural, very religious notions when thinking of how God speaks to us?

We always want the magical – the transcendent and the earth shattering – where the voice of God is concerned. And then, when the voice of God does come, we then expect for the "Word" to be confirmed at least three times from other prophets before we even think about beginning to accept that the word was valid and true. My friend this is not how faith truly operates. This is not what "knowing" looks like within the Kingdom of God. And, above all, this is not how God operates within our lives. Not only is the voice of God very natural, but the voice of God is also much more effortless than most of religion would ever dare to admit. Communion with God isn't some "dog and pony show." It's very real. It ebbs and flows. It's conversational. It's natural. And, above all else, it is unmistakable. Yes, true communion with God through the inner leading of the Holy Spirit is undeniable and unmistakable.

It's time to rethink the true meaning of communication with God and begin to harness the power and the authority that you've been entrusted with as a believer and a seeker. Jesus said that those who seek will always find – meaning that there is a very real answer and a very real end-result that awaits all who ask. Unfortunately, where religion is so often concerned, there's the faulty premise that suggests we're going to be left always waiting, always hoping, and always seeking. No. Jesus said that not only will those who seek be given the opportunity to find but that to them that knock, doorways will always become opened. Right now, even in this moment, there is a realm of infinite possibilities existing for you – a world of limitless potential that's yours for the asking and the receiving. To obtain this realm, though, requires that you begin to change your mind and shift your perspective where hearing from God is concerned.

Strengthen your belief system. Change your perspective from "I hope to hear God" to "I *know* I hear God." Believe me, you'll be pleasantly surprised to find that when you do, not only will you begin to build a greater sense of confidence within your faith but you will, in turn, begin to develop an even greater boldness, approaching the throne of God with boldness and assuming your rightful place within the Kingdom of Heaven. Communion with Heaven isn't simply a blessing you've been granted; it is a fundamental birthright in the Kingdom of

God. And until you recognize that you have a right to communicate with God, you will forever be left tossed about by the winds of ever-changing religious doctrines. It's time to lay claim to your birthright. Communication with God is that birthright!

"And seeing a fig tree afar off having leaves, he came, if haply he might find any thing thereon: and when he came to it, he found nothing but leaves; for the time of figs was not yet. And Jesus answered and said unto it, No man eat fruit of thee hereafter for ever. And his disciples heard it. And they come to Jerusalem: and Jesus went into the temple, and began to cast out them that sold and bought in the temple, and overthrew the tables of the moneychangers, and the seats of them that sold doves; And would not suffer that any man should carry any vessel through the temple. And he taught, saying unto them, Is it not written, My house shall be called

of all nations the house of prayer? but ye have made it a den of thieves. And the scribes and chief priests heard it, and sought how they might destroy him: for they feared him, because all the people was astonished at his doctrine. And when even was come, he went out of the city. And in the morning, as they passed by, they saw the fig tree dried up from the roots. And Peter calling to remembrance saith unto him, Master, behold, the fig tree which thou cursedst is withered away. And Jesus answering saith unto them, Have faith in God. For verily I say unto you, That whosoever shall say unto this mountain, Be thou removed, and be thou cast into the sea; and shall not doubt in his heart, but shall believe that those things which he saith shall come to pass; he shall have whatsoever he saith. Therefore I say unto you, What things soever ye desire, when ye pray, believe that ye receive them, and ye shall have them. And when ye stand praying, forgive, if ye have ought against any: that your Father also which is in heaven may forgive you your trespasses. But if ye do not forgive, neither will your Father which is in heaven forgive your trespasses. And they come again to Jerusalem: and as he was walking in the temple, there come to him the chief priests, and the scribes, and the elders, And say unto him, By what authority doest thou these things? and who gave thee this authority to do these things? And Jesus answered and said unto them, I will also ask of you one question, and answer me, and I will tell you by what authority I do these things. The baptism of John, was it from heaven, or of men? answer me. And they reasoned with themselves, saying, If we shall say, From heaven; he will say, Why then did ye not believe him? But if we shall say, Of men; they feared the people: for all men counted John, that he was a prophet indeed. And they answered and said unto Jesus, We cannot tell. And Jesus answering saith unto them, Neither do I tell you by what authority I do these things." (Mark 11:13-33 KJV)

The authority you possess to bring the realm of Heaven into the physical dimension of Earth will forever be tied to what you believe about your communication with God in everyday life. Whether you realize it or not, in this moment, the extent of your communication with God is intrinsically interwoven into your belief system, and what you believe about prayer and the prophetic is directly determining the outcome of your communication. To hear from God more clearly and more accurately, believe that you can and that you do. Your belief is the catalyst which propels you into greater clarity and greater understanding. Hear me when I say, there is no "maybe" in the Kingdom of Heaven. It simply doesn't work that way. Not only will you and I be given what we believe, but we will be given exactly what we believe. It's time to change the way you think about the power you truly possess. And, as you will see and begin to discover, with a shift of perspective, even greater communication is made possible.

You don't have to live life feeling as though you're always "missing it." You don't have to live a life of uncertainty, always questioning and always going about with a sense of inferiority. You've been given a blessed assurance that you can not only communicate with God but that your beliefs and your thoughts are constantly creating the paradigms of your life. If you truly desire to take your communication with God to a new level, begin by believing that it is already so. Believing, after all, is truly the only battle you've ever really been called to fight. It's time to fight against those old paradigms of self-limiting, self-defeating beliefs, and it's time to harness the power you've been given. It's time to make communication with the realm of

Heaven a more natural part of your everyday life experience. And when you do, not only will you unleash the power you truly possess within the Kingdom, but you will manifest the Kingdom of God in the realm of Earth in a greater, more powerful way than ever before.

CHAPTER THREE

A LASTING INTIMACY

Not only are you in a covenantal agreement with the Creator, but you are in the most intimate relationship of all – union with God. And with this union also come certain unalienable rights. Within the union of lasting intimacy, there are certain benefits which exist for those who believe and for those who diligently seek after the voice of God – those who cherish the voice of God above all else. As with any relationship built upon intimacy, there is a sense of passionate pursuit involved. Within the Kingdom, though, the very things that we pursue in God are always the very things that are pursuing us. Suffice it to say, there's a reason you've always had such a hunger for the voice of the LORD within your life. There's a reason you've always been so drawn to the prophetic gift. It isn't because you're weird or into extreme things, contrary to what your friends and family may have said. The reason, quite simply, is because the voice of God has always been calling out to you first.

It wasn't that long ago that a woman named Melissa contacted the offices of Identity Network to inquire of the Word of the LORD for her life. Like everyone, Melissa had questions about the direction of her life – in many ways, the questions that we all find ourselves asking from time to time. Like many, Melissa had spent most of her life battling insecurity. She had faced that pain of multiple abusive relationships – relationships that served only to further diminish her self-esteem. Religion never seemed to help. In fact, due to years of religious programming, not only did Melissa feel that she had to work to earn the love of people; she also felt as though she had to always work to earn the love of God. As simple as the question may seem, she asked, "Does God love me?" At first glance, such a question may seem quite elementary; however, for someone battling crippling insecurity and a debilitating sense of inferiority, such a question comes from a genuine heart.

"I believe God loves me, but I just need to be sure I'm hearing God clearly," Melissa said. In the prophetic reading, so much validation and so much unconditional love came – a love so overwhelming that it shook me to my core as I shared the Word of the LORD for her. But it didn't seem to be enough. She asked, "But how can I be sure this is true? How can I be sure that God really loves me as much as you're saying?" I explained that, with all things, a step of faith is demanded of believers and that to move from the place of uncertainty to the realm of assurance we must begin to come to the place of knowing within our thoughts and within our minds. But it didn't seem to be enough. Doubt and unbelief seemed to continue to grip her.

I share this very real, very practical example with you to say that it's all too common to relate our relationship to God to our relationship with people, here in the realm of Earth – relegating our expectations of God to the expectations of humans. Here in the physical realm of Earth, when you have a breakup or a moment of trauma in an earthly, human relationship, typically the very first thing to end is the element of communication. When someone disappoints you, you simply stop talking to them. When a husband or wife, even in a marriage relationship, becomes frustrated or angered, all too often communication is withheld. In fact, when was the last time you withheld communication from someone in your life simply because you were frustrated, agitated or even annoyed? All too often, we place these same beliefs upon our relationship with the Creator, believing all too often that God will simply withhold communication because He's angry or because we've in some way disappointed Him. Communication with God, though, is not a human concept. It's greater. It's much more transcendent.

The ways of God are not our ways, and His thoughts and His ways are much higher than our own ways, as the scriptures continuously bear out. When we consider the voice of God, it's important that we recognize that we are speaking of a deeper, more inward, spiritual work. We're speaking of the realm of soul and spirit – not the realm of natural, human emotion stemming from the natural, carnal, religious mind. It's time to go deeper into the recesses of who you truly are if you are ever going to learn to hear the voice of God for yourself with greater accuracy and precision. God is Spirit, and those who come to God must do so by the Spirit and not through human, natural emotion – from the perspective of temporal, often shallow, fickle emotion. As the scriptures declare, those who come to God must first believe that He is and that He is a rewarder of all who diligently seeker after Him. It's time to look higher and to go deeper.

The Kingdom begins within, as Jesus said. Chances are, even as you read these words, to some degree you're feeling some level of abandonment within your own personal life – perhaps in your career or with friends or even in your marriage. Chances are, right now, communication with those you love most may seem rocky, at best. Perhaps you've gone through very real, very literal moments of abandonment – the divorce, the abuse, the unexpected loss of the job that you were devoted to for decades. All of these moments of abandonment, though, have happened upon the natural, human level – in human interactions. The ways of God are much higher and much deeper. To better hear the voice of God within your own life, you're going to have to begin to understand more fully that God isn't seeking to abandon you and that in those moments in which it feels the voice of God is distant or far-off, God isn't withholding His voice to be malicious or to somehow prove a point. No. Even in the moments that feel as though God is withholding His voice, even then, the responsibility to hear God clearly rests upon the seeker – not upon God. God is always speaking.

There is no greater intimacy than the love of God for His Creation. In fact, the Kingdom of Heaven and also the mechanics by which the Kingdom operates can best be summed up in lasting intimacy. It is love – it is intimacy – which fuels communication with Heaven and with the heavenly realms. To better understand and to better, more accurately discern the voice of God within your own life and to awaken your own prophetic gift all the more, you're going to have to begin to know that God loves you. God, after all, *is* love. Knowing this, then, it is safe to assert that all communication with Heaven is grounded and rooted in love alone. God isn't vengeful, isn't malicious, or wrathful, as religion claims. Even in your moments of human abandonment, Haven has been calling out to you in an attempt to awaken you to the power of spiritual communication with Heaven. And even in those moments of earthly, human pain and suffering, the voice of God has not been distant or far off.

The Lord is near. But just exactly how near is He? The answer may surprise you. The ancient writers of old seemed to understand that the voice of God is somehow unmovable – unshakable. They seemed to have an understanding that even in the midst of human trial and suffering – even in the midst of daily, human activities – the voice of God is always present. To better understand this, though, requires a more proper, more comprehensive understanding that God actually wants to communicate. He desires communication above all else. And even in the moments when it seems as though the voice of God is being withheld, even then, the Spirit is always speaking within, in the deeper realm of the soul and spirit.

John 10:27 declares, *"My sheep hear my voice, and I know them, and they follow me."* In Romans 10:17, the Apostle Paul states, *"So then faith [cometh] by hearing, and hearing by the word of God."* The Word of the LORD through the Prophet Jeremiahs, in Jeremiah 33:3, declares, *"Call unto me, and I will answer thee, and shew thee great and mighty things, which thou knowest not."* Jesus, in John 8:47 declares, *"He that is of God heareth God's words: ye therefore hear [them] not, because ye are not of God."* And countless other scriptures abound. *"And thine ears shall hear a word behind thee, saying, This [is] the way, walk ye in it, when ye turn to the right hand, and when ye turn to the left." (Isaiah 30:21 KJV) "Howbeit when he, the Spirit of truth, is come, he will guide you into all truth: for he shall not speak of himself;*

but whatsoever he shall hear, [that] shall he speak: and he will shew you things to come." (John 16:13 KJV) "But he said, Yea rather, blessed [are] they that hear the word of God, and keep it." (Luke 11:28 KJV) "For the word of God [is] quick, and powerful, and sharper than any twoedged sword, piercing even to the dividing asunder of soul and spirit, and of the joints and marrow, and [is] a discerner of the thoughts and intents of the heart" (Hebrews 4:12 KJV). "It is the spirit that quickeneth; the flesh profiteth nothing: the words that I speak unto you, [they] are spirit, and [they] are life." (John 6:63 KJV) "But the Comforter, [which is] the Holy Ghost, whom the Father will send in my name, he shall teach you all things, and bring all things to your remembrance, whatsoever I have said unto you." (John 14:26 KJV) "Therefore we ought to give the more earnest heed to the things which we have heard, lest at any time we should let [them] slip."

(Hebrews 2:1 KJV) *"For as many as are led by the Spirit of God, they are the sons of God."* *(Romans 8:14 KJV)*

Yet, through the scriptures, through every illustration of the voice of God coming to humanity, we see a common theme recurring: the power of the Spirit. We are reminded that it is only through the Spirit – through the inner Kingdom – that we can correctly hear and correctly discern the voice of God within our own daily lives. And so what do these statements truly mean for us? Are we, being human, simply destined to always struggle and always fight to have to hear the voice of God clearly and accurately? Are we, being human and living upon Planet Earth, destined to always have to wonder and have to guess if we're hearing God clearly? Or is there some greater truth that must be recognized? I would respectfully submit that the scriptures, in fact, are true and that God is always speaking. To understand this though requires that, as Paul stated, the eyes of our understanding become enlightened.

When we speak of intimacy with God, we aren't speaking solely of a mere closeness – the type of closeness that we find in even our closest human interactions. No. In fact, we are speaking of an intimacy that even far surpasses and far supersedes the most lasting intimacy that we know here within the realm of flesh. We are speaking of a closeness – of an intimacy – that is always present and always working within us, even beyond the realm of natural human emotion and thought. When we speak of the voice of God, we are speaking of an inner work. After all, as Jesus continuously taught throughout his earthly life and ministry, the Kingdom of Heaven is an inner, deeper realm which supersedes and far surpasses the natural world.

Right now, even as you read these words, the Kingdom is in full operation within you and through you. Right now, even as you read these words, the Kingdom is permeating literally every fiber of your being, radiating outwardly and spilling over onto the tapestry of your human experience. If the scriptures are true and all things truly do work together for good, then it's quite safe to assume that the Kingdom is always working at all times continuously. What does this truly reveal for the seeker such as you? It means that at no time were you ever without the voice of God within your life. Never have you been separated from the voice of the Holy Spirit because of the Kingdom within you.

That means, even more practically speaking, that you were hearing God even in the midst of the divorce. You were hearing God even during the loss of your job. You were hearing God even when it seemed that you weren't. It means that even when you received the diagnosis from the doctor that placed fear in your heart, even then you were in a position to hear from God. Even in those most painful and most traumatic moments, God was speaking and you, even then, possessed the ability to hear. The only issue was, at times, you didn't discern clearly. There were times when you rushed to judgment too quickly. There were times when you acted too hastily and without much thought. There were times when you made moves based upon feelings that were temporal. However, it cannot be stressed enough that even in those moments of trial and testing – those very traumatic moments of life – even then you were hearing from God. Communication with Heaven never ceased. It never ended. It never stopped.

The fact that the scriptures speak of the voice of God as a continuous and ever-present reality within the lives of men and women seems to suggest that in order to better understand the mechanics of Spirit communication and in order to better, more clearly discern the voice of the Holy Spirit within, one must, in fact, begin to look *within*. It's time to go deeper. It's time to transcend and to begin to view the voice of God as what it truly is! It is an inner voice, stemming from an inner reality! However, the inner reality is always confirming itself in all aspects of daily, natural, physical life! What's within you is continuously trying to get your attention in all matters of daily life – when you're driving to work, when you're having conversations with friends, and, yes even when you're feeling so isolated, so lonely, and so separated from the voice of God. All of life is speaking to you! All of Heaven wants to make itself known to you – right now in the here and now!

When I began to realize all those years ago within my own life that the realm of Heaven isn't simply an inner reality but that it is, in fact, always operating around me just as much as it is operating within me and through me, it began to change the way that I viewed communication with God. I realized that, although religion never seems to recognize it, God is not only speaking to me about my life; God is speaking to me through my life! My friend and fellow seeker, I promise you that when you grab hold of this revelation, never again will you ever feel separated or disconnected from the voice of God. In fact, by realizing that God is speaking to you through all matters of daily life, never again will you ever even feel the need to question whether or not you're hearing His voice. Confidence will begin to replace doubt and unbelief and a sense of certainty will cause all questioning to give way to a sense of inner knowing. I don't think I hear from God; I know I hear from God!

As with all things concerning the Kingdom, though, a much needed shift of perspective is needed in order to recognize God clearly. The scriptures remind us to "taste and see" that the LORD is good! Well, it's impossible to taste and to see without the use of natural, physical senses. And so what does this truly suggest to us, as seekers and as believers? It suggests that we're able to experience God within all matters of natural, physical, daily life! And it reminds us that even while we're here in this present world and even while we're experiencing life upon Planet Earth that it is possible to hear God clearly and accurately! We're reminded that the voice of God is equally just as natural as it is spiritual. It's just as practical as it is transcendent because the Kingdom is in operation not just within us and through us but also all around us!

All throughout his earthly life and ministry, Jesus continuously taught concerning the Kingdom of Heaven. In fact, the truth of the matter is that it was the only thing he ever taught – encouraging believers and seekers to experience the realm of Heaven here on Earth as it is in the realm of the Holy Spirit. Even when Jesus taught us to pray, the prayer was for Heaven to be revealed upon the Earth. Think of that for a moment. Imagine what such a teaching truly means! Rather than waiting for some spiritual experience by which to hear the voice of God, it's possible to experience the realm of Heaven in all matter so daily life – here in the natural! The Gospel, in fact, is the message of the Kingdom. When Jesus preached and even when he sent the disciples to preach, only one, singular message was shared: the Gospel of the Kingdom. The Gospel is, in fact, the message of the inner Kingdom. And the "Good News" is that Heaven has always been within you the entire time!

"And when he was demanded of the Pharisees, when the kingdom of God should come, he answered them and said, The kingdom of God cometh not with observation: Neither shall they say, Lo here! or, lo there! for, behold, the kingdom of God is within you. And he said unto the disciples, The days will come, when ye shall desire to see one of the days of the Son of man, and ye shall not see it. And they shall say to you, See here; or, see there: go not after them, nor follow them. For as the lightning, that lighteneth out of the one part under heaven, shineth unto the other part under heaven; so shall also the Son of man be in his day. But first must he suffer many things, and be rejected of

this generation." (Luke 17:20-25 KJV) The Kingdom of Heaven is a present, inner reality. And never has it ever been apart from you. When you begin to realize that God is always, at all times, not only speaking to you but is always, always speaking through you, never again will you question your ability to hear from Heaven.

CHAPTER FOUR

BORN OF THE SPIRIT

T he voice of God isn't something that you hear; it's something that you know. The scriptures make it plain that to even see or to hear the things of God, there must be a renewal of the soul, by the Spirit. There must be a rebirth, of sorts. This rebirth is a shift of perspective. It's repentance. Contrary to the teachings of religion, though, repentance simply means to "shift" within the mind. I felt led to include this chapter within the book because I want to encourage you to adapt your thinking to a better sense of knowing. I want you to realize and begin to understand more fully just how close – just how near – the voice of God is to you. Surprisingly, it's much closer than you think. Yet, ironically, it's also just as close as you think because everything within the Kingdom is enacted through thought and through belief, just as Jesus said.

When Jesus spoke to Nicodemus concerning the things of God, he spoke of a rebirth. Nicodemus, marveling at the words, mistakenly thought that Jesus was referring to natural things – a natural, physical rebirth. Jesus explained to him that rebirth is spiritual in nature. But within the words of Jesus we find something truly remarkable concerning the realm of the Holy Spirit and the, yes, even concerning the voice of God. We find that when a shift of perspective – a change of thinking – comes, that we are able to interact within Heaven in new and exciting ways. In fact, in the words of Jesus to Nicodemus, we find great symbolism of the realm of Heaven even being within the natural, three-dimensional world even when we aren't fully aware of it. Consider the words of Jesus to Nicodemus as a sort of behind-the-scenes glimpse into the mechanics of the spiritual realms, giving insight into how the realm of the Holy Spirit truly operates within our lives – and within the realm of the Earth.

"There was a man of the Pharisees, named Nicodemus, a ruler of the Jews: The same came to Jesus by night, and said unto him, Rabbi, we know that thou art a teacher come from God: for no man can do these miracles that thou doest, except God be with him. Jesus answered and said unto him, Verily, verily, I say unto thee, Except a man be born again, he cannot see the kingdom of God. Nicodemus saith unto him, How can a man be born when he is old? can he

enter the second time into his mother's womb, and be born? Jesus answered, Verily, verily, I say unto thee, Except a man be born of water and of the Spirit, he cannot enter into the kingdom of God. That which is born of the flesh is flesh; and that which is born of the Spirit is spirit. Marvel not that I said unto thee, Ye must be born again. The wind bloweth where it listeth, and thou hearest the sound thereof, but canst not tell whence it cometh, and whither it goeth: so is every one that is born of the Spirit. Nicodemus answered and said unto him, How can these things be? Jesus answered and said unto him, Art thou a master of Israel, and knowest not these things? Verily, verily, I say unto thee, We speak that we do know, and testify that we have seen; and ye receive not our witness. If I have told you earthly things, and ye believe not, how shall ye believe, if I tell you of heavenly things? And no man hath ascended up to heaven, but he that came down from heaven, *even the Son of man which is in heaven. And as Moses lifted up the serpent in the wilderness, even so must the Son of man be lifted up: That whosoever believeth in him should not perish, but have eternal life. For God so loved the world, that he gave his only begotten Son, that whosoever believeth in him should not perish, but have everlasting life. For God sent not his Son into the world to condemn the world; but that the world through him might be saved. He that believeth on him is not condemned: but he that believeth not is condemned already, because he hath not believed in the name of the only begotten Son of God. And this is the condemnation, that light is come into the world, and men loved darkness rather than light, because their deeds were evil. For every one that doeth evil hateth the light, neither cometh to the light, lest his deeds should be reproved. But he that doeth truth cometh to the light, that his deeds may be made manifest, that they are wrought in God." (John 3:1-21 KJV)*

Notice that within the words of Jesus to Nicodemus, we're given a glimpse into the realm of Heaven and shown a very startling truth: when the mind is renewed, we begin to see the realm of the Holy Spirit all around us! When the mind is shifted and born of the Spirit, we become able to see the Presence of God in operation even within the realm of physical Earth and become able to better hear the voice of God in all matters of daily life. When Jesus spoke of the wind rustling through the trees, comparing the wind to the Presence of God, he wasn't simply using an analogy. In fact, if you were to study the scriptures, you would find that wind and breath have always been indicative of the Presence of the Holy Spirit – even in various other world religions throughout history. Jesus was emphatically saying that if you want to experience the realm of Heaven on Earth and truly desire to hear the voice of God clearly you're going to have to shift your perspective until you're able to see and to hear God here within the natural world!

Oh how I pray that you would grab hold of this revelation! I promise you, my fellow seeker, that the moment you begin to shift your perspective and begin to repent – to "turn within your mind" – not only will you begin to access greater clarity within the Kingdom of God but you will, in turn, begin to see God and to hear God in often the most unlikely of places even here within the physical world. What if you could see that God is always speaking to His Creation, through His Creation? Would such a revelation not only change the way the Body of Christ views the concept of prayer but also serve to awaken humanity to the truth of the realm of the Holy Spirit? The Creator is not only speaking to his Creation; He is speaking through His Creation. And you, my fellow seeker, are the crowning jewel of all Creation. You've been elevated within the dimension of Heaven to be seated with Him in heavenly places – even in the here and now!

Jesus said that his sheep "know" his voice. Again, the voice of God isn't something that one simply hears; the voice of God is something that one knows at the deepest level – at the core of their innermost being. The original word for "know," in the original language of the scriptures is the term "YADA." YADA, though, has a meaning that far supersedes and far surpasses a mere knowing "within the mind." In order to better understand what it means to know the voice of God, it's important to have a better understanding of Jesus's true intentions when he spoke of this sense of "knowing." Was he merely speaking of a certain sense of inner recognition, or was he speaking of something more? As I've said for years, when studying the ancient text of the scriptures, it's vital that we understand not only the origin of the text but also the language used. Far too often, we rely solely upon religious interpretation when examining the text and, all too often, as a result, we're left with a shallow understanding, not correctly dividing the Word of Truth. "Knowing" refers to a far greater depth of intimacy.

Harken back, if you will, to other accounts within the scriptures: the account in which the angel Gabriel announces to Mary that she will conceive and bring forth a child and call his name "Jesus" and also the words of Jesus when he claims that "on the last day" many will be told "Depart from me; I never knew you." Interestingly enough – shockingly, in fact – in both of these instances, we find in the original text the usage of the term "YADA," referring to a greater sense of intimacy. Of course Mary "knew" other male figures within her life. She had never been intimate with a man, though. "YADA" refers to a sexual intimacy – an intimacy so deep and so all-encompassing that it leads to rebirth and, most of all, to "reproduction. Knowing this, we find that the voice of God is not only something that exists upon a much deeper level but also that the voice of God serves a very real purpose. The voice of God serves to produce and to reproduce something within the realm of Earth!

"And in the sixth month the angel Gabriel was sent from God unto a city of Galilee, named Nazareth, To a virgin espoused to a man whose name was Joseph, of the house of David; and the virgin's name was Mary. And the angel came in unto her, and said, Hail, thou that art highly favoured, the Lord is with thee: blessed

art thou among women. And when she saw him, she was troubled at his saying, and cast in her mind what manner of salutation this should be. And the angel said unto her, Fear not, Mary: for thou hast found favour with God. And, behold, thou shalt conceive in thy womb, and bring forth a son, and shalt call his name Jesus. He shall be great, and shall be called the Son of the Highest: and the Lord God shall give unto him the throne of his father David: And he shall reign over the house of Jacob for ever; and of his kingdom there shall be no end. Then said Mary unto the angel, How shall this be, seeing I know not a man?" (Luke 1:26-34 KJV)

More shockingly, though, in the words of Jesus, we find perhaps the greatest glimpse into power of this knowing, when he speaks of all that we are to accomplish within the Kingdom of God while in the realm of Earth. *"Enter ye in at the strait gate: for wide is the gate, and broad is the way, that leadeth to destruction, and many there be which go in thereat: Because strait is the gate, and narrow is the way, which leadeth unto life, and few there be that find it. Beware of false prophets, which come to you in sheep's clothing, but inwardly they are ravening wolves. Ye shall know them by their fruits. Do men gather grapes of thorns, or figs of thistles? Even so every good tree bringeth forth good fruit; but a corrupt tree bringeth forth evil fruit. A good tree cannot bring forth evil fruit, neither can a corrupt tree bring forth good fruit. Every tree that bringeth not forth good fruit is hewn down, and cast into the fire. Wherefore by their fruits ye shall know them. Not every one that saith unto me, Lord, Lord, shall enter into the kingdom of heaven; but he that doeth the will of my Father which is in heaven. Many will say to me in that day, Lord, Lord, have we not prophesied in thy name? and in thy name have cast out devils? and in thy name done many*

wonderful works? And then will I profess unto them, I never knew you: depart from me, ye that work iniquity. Therefore whosoever heareth these sayings of mine, and doeth them, I will liken him unto a wise man, which built his house upon a rock: And the rain descended, and the floods came, and the winds blew, and beat upon that house; and it fell not: for it was founded upon a rock. And every one that heareth these sayings of mine, and doeth them not, shall be likened unto a foolish man, which built his house upon the sand: And the rain descended, and the floods came, and the winds blew, and beat upon that house; and it fell: and great was the fall of it. And it came to pass, when Jesus had ended these sayings, the people were astonished at his doctrine: For he taught them as one having authority, and not as the scribes."
(Matthew 7:13-29 KJV)

In both of these passages, we find the term "knowing" to mean something much, much more transcendent than just a mere inner, recognition. We find that "knowing" refers to sexual intimacy – an intimacy that leads to reproduction. When Jesus spoke of those who would claim to have accomplished much for the Kingdom, he alludes to the fact that there would be those who were never truly "known" – that the Christ had never truly been reproduced within them and through them. In other words, to put it more plainly, there would be those who would possess a form of godliness but deny the power. And so, how does this relate to the voice of God within our lives? In fact, it relates in every single way imaginable! The voice of God is not something that is merely "known" within the mind; the voice of God is something that must take root and then lead to reproduction within the realm of Earth! The voice of God, though heavenly and spiritual, must be brought forth into the physical realm. And it does so the moment you recognize the voice of God as a deep intimate certainty rather than as some religious thing.

You're pregnant with the voice of God and the voice of God is your solemn, sacred birthright. Communication with Heaven is a right that all who live and walk upon this planet possess. In the words of Jesus, we find that knowing is the greatest, most deepest form of intimacy that exists. How much more deeply then is the voice of God within all who live? To better understand the correlation between "knowing" and the voice of God, let us then examine the words of Jesus in the synoptic Gospel of John. *"My sheep hear my voice, and I know them, and they follow me: And I give unto them eternal life; and they shall never perish, neither shall any man pluck them out of my hand." (John 10:27-28 KJV)*

Notice that in the words of Jesus, the same term is used: "YADA." The sheep do not simply believe in the voice of God. They don't merely hear the voice; they know the voice of God – intimately. My friend and fellow seeker, you could not escape the voice of God in your life even if you wanted! It's impossible! Every fiber of your being even here within the physical world and, indeed, literally all Creation, has been infused with the very essence of the voice of God and there is no separating the Presence of God from the Creation of God. By divine and intelligent design, you are even now hearing the voice of God within you as you read these words. With each and every passing thought, you are harnessing the power of spiritual communication with Heaven and are, as a result, communing with God even when the natural, carnal, more religious mind isn't fully aware of it!

You are infused with the Presence of God. You're pregnant with the inner voice because the Kingdom of Heaven is within you. And, the more you begin to realize that the voice of God is already within you, the more clearly, the more accurately you will be able to discern the voice of God speaking within. When you move from the place of mere believing to the realm of absolute knowing, never again will you view the voice of God as something far-off or distant. Instead, you will begin to see that even the most difficult and most painful moments of your life have been the voice of God manifesting within you and through you the entire time, all along! When knowing comes, the Kingdom is made more clear. When knowing comes, so too does the abundant life. And after all, is that not the promise we have in Him?

CHAPTER FIVE

TRUE SPIRITUALITY

We're always fighting against ourselves in this life – always believing that to be human and to be within the natural, physical world means that we must, by our very human nature – somehow be separated from God. Jesus came, though, to not only atone for humanity but to end the war that humanity constantly rages within itself. Your humanity in no way separates you from God, and it's time you begin to realize it. Your humanity, in fact, is just one of the many, many ways in which the voice of God speaks and also one of the many, many ways in which God draws you to Himself. Religion has always, always had an uncanny way of fueling war – spiritual wars as well as natural wars. Chances are, even this week, you've heard accounts of men and women killing or causing harm to others or even protesting with hateful words – shockingly, all in the name of God. The wars that we see in the natural world, though, have always, always come from the wars that we wage within our own selves. There is nothing more deadly or more damnable than the lies of religion. God hates it.

It's time to stop fighting against your humanity so that you can finally learn to better recognize God speaking to you all throughout the day and night. You've, I'm sure, become all too familiar with these inner wars that we fight if you've ever even considered the voice of God at any time in your life. The wars go a little something like this: "That's not God." "God would never say that." "Surely, God would never speak like that." "That doesn't seem like God to me." Even more practically, perhaps, the wars sound a little something like this: "That must have been the Devil." "The Devil made me do it." "They aren't hearing from God." "They're being deceived to have beliefs like that." "They're wrong." All of these statements represent an inner war – and a very real spiritual war.

As I've said for years, it was never the plan of God for you to be in the army your entire life – always fighting, always waging war, and always, always looking for some fight in the name of God. Who exactly are you fighting against, other than your very own self? The Devil? Surely not. Demons? Surely not. After all, as the scriptures make perfectly clear it was for this cause that the Son of God was made manifested that He might destroy the works of the Devil. Religion is not only deadly but evil not because of legalism or ritualistic practice but, more so, because of its own hypocrisy. Has it ever occurred to you that perhaps the Body of Christ always seems to fight and wage war against itself – and others – simply because it doesn't really believe? Religion doesn't believe in the finished work of Christ that way it claims and it never really has. It's all just a smokescreen used to control and to manipulate the masses.

If you believe in the work of Christ then you stop fighting wars against your own self and wars against those unlike you – those who seem different than you. Again, all war stems from the wars we wage against our very own selves. For centuries, religion has erroneously claimed that to be human is to in some way be, by definition, un-spiritual. It simply isn't true, and the fact of the matter is that it's never really been the case at all. But what are we to make of the many statements within the New Testament regarding the war between the spirit and the flesh? What are we to make the Pauline Epistles – the writings in which Paul emphatically states that even when he seeks to do good that evil is always present within him? Are we to simply dismiss such statements? Are we to simply selectively choose certain passages of text to fit our narrative? Of course not. But we do have to mature in our understanding and have the eyes of our understanding enlightened. We do have to grow up in God.

What if you've been thinking about God – and about yourself – all wrong, all along? What if, rather than being at war with God by your very humanity, you could begin to recognize that you truly have been created and crafted in the very image and in the very likeness of God? You've heard that, I'm sure. Chances are, to some small degree you probably even know that at some deep level within. But do you truly believe it enough for it to permeate your life to the point that it changes your perception? That, my friend, is the true battle. I stopped fighting myself years ago, and, shockingly, it was then and only then that I began to hear the voice of God more clearly for myself. Do you truly desire to hear the voice of God? If so, lose your religion.

The Kingdom of Heaven is alive and active and working through you, just as Jesus said. It's inescapable! It cannot be separated from your life because it is an ever-present reality. But not only is the Kingdom of Heaven operating within you and through you, but it is operating also throughout all Creation around you! Most people don't realize that the answers to questions come as Creation awakens – meaning that the answers we seek are always, always continuously unfolding around us like a flower opening. By now, as you've read these words and have journeyed with me deeper into this revelation concerning the reality of the voice of God, I'm sure that by now we've noticed that we're building a case – a case that the voice of Gods is natural and is in operation all around you. Did you know that even the natural world is serving to remind you always, at all times of the power of the realm of the spiritual world of Heaven? It's true!

When Paul spoke of the "evil" being present within him, he wasn't speaking of evil as we within the modern world sometimes view the concept of evil. After all, as the scriptures make perfectly clear, what fellowship can light have with darkness? In order to better understand and to come to a more comprehensive understanding of the spiritual and the natural world, it's important to understand that Paul was always peaking of the natural, human perception being the enemy of God – not humanity itself and not the human flesh. He was speaking, rather, of the eyes of our understanding and of the need to awaken within our minds, having the mind renewed so that it could learn to better *see* and to *hear* the things of the God within the realm of natural Earth. Do you really, truly believe for even one moment that the Apostle Paul was evil? Certainly not! And so, when he spoke of the flesh waging war against the Spirit, he wasn't speaking of the natural flesh; he was speaking of the natural mind!

"Therefore seeing we have this ministry, as we have received mercy, we faint not; But have renounced the hidden things of dishonesty, not walking in craftiness, nor handling the word of God deceitfully; but by manifestation of the truth commending ourselves to every man's

conscience in the sight of God. But if our gospel be hid, it is hid to them that are lost: In whom the god of this world hath blinded the minds of them which believe not, lest the light of the glorious gospel of Christ, who is the image of God, should shine unto them. For we preach not ourselves, but Christ Jesus the Lord; and ourselves your servants for Jesus' sake. For God, who commanded the light to shine out of darkness, hath shined in our hearts, to give the light of the knowledge of the glory of God in the face of Jesus Christ. But we have this treasure in earthen vessels, that the excellency of the power may be of God, and not of us. We are troubled on every side, yet not distressed; we are perplexed, but not in despair; Persecuted, but not forsaken; cast down, but not destroyed; Always bearing about in the body the dying of the Lord Jesus, that the life also of Jesus might be made manifest in our body. For we which live are always delivered unto death for Jesus' sake, that the life also of Jesus might be made manifest in our mortal flesh. So then death worketh in us, but life in you. We having the same spirit of faith, according as it is written, I believed, and therefore have I spoken; we also believe, and therefore speak; Knowing that he which raised up the Lord Jesus shall raise up us also by Jesus, and shall present us with you. For all things are for your sakes, that the abundant grace might through the thanksgiving of many redound to the glory of God. For which cause we faint not; but though our outward man perish, yet the inward man is renewed day by day. For our light affliction, which is but for a moment, worketh for us a far more exceeding and eternal weight of glory; While we look not at the things which are seen, but at the things which are not seen: for the things which are seen are temporal; but the things which are not seen are eternal." (2 Corinthians 4:1-18 KJV)

Notice that within the passage, Paul specifically states that the things which are seen have come from the things which are not seen and that the things which are not seen are the eternal things. Recognizing this, it becomes much easier to understand the perspective of the early first century church where the voice of God is concerned. The early church and even the apostles believed firmly that God was speaking not in spite of the natural world but rather in sync with the natural world! Oh, how I pray that you would receive this revelation, my fellow seeker! The moment that you could begin to grasp that not only is God speaking to Creation but that God is speaking through Creation, never again will you ever feel the need to judge or condemn yourself. As the scriptures declare, there is no more condemnation to those in Christ who walk after the things of the Spirit!

And if this above text wasn't enough to illustrate the belief of the early church concerning the voice of God, the scriptures also speak of all Creation groaning and crying out in an attempt to get the attention of humanity! Did you know that even Creation and, yes, even the created things are being used by God to get your attention? It's true! Even the natural, physical world is groaning and crying out at all times in an effort to declare the glory and the majesty of God! And so, what are we to make to make of spirituality and prayer and hearing the voice of God, particularly where the words of the Apostle Paul and various other texts are concerned? The answer, quite simply, is that even within the natural, physical world, the voice of God is real and is always present! There's a reason the Holy Spirit inspired me to entitle this book "The Three-Dimensional Ways." The reason is because the voice of God is literally three-dimensional in nature! Not only is God speaking within you but God is speaking all around you as well.

As the Gospel of John states, in the Beginning was the Word, and the very Word was God Himself – meaning that all things which were created were created by the very Word and by the voice of Almighty God. How then would it even be possible to separate Creation from the voice of God when all of Creation has emanated from that voice to begin with? It's impossible! The voice of God is not only existing in the spiritual dimension within but it is also existing in the very real three-dimensional world without, externally also. By learning to recognize the voice of God as a reality not in spite of the world but also through the natural world, working in the midst of the natural world, you will not only begin to develop a greater sensitivity to the voice of God but you will, in turn, also begin to see God everywhere you go! And is that not what the Kingdom truly means here within the natural realm of Earth?

Jesus, being the great reconciler that he is, has reconciled the world to God! Sure, you've I'm sure heard this statement made for decades. However, unfortunately, the Body of Christ all too often fails to consider what such a statement might truly mean. If Christ has redeemed the world unto Himself, then would it not stand to reason that Christ is also being revealed within the world, through all matters of daily life happening all around you? Your humanity has not served to separate you from God. It is only serving to attempt to remind you to become more God-conscious – more open to seeing the glory of God within the realm of Earth.

"There is therefore now no condemnation to them which are in Christ Jesus, who walk not after the flesh, but after the Spirit. For the law of the Spirit of life in Christ Jesus hath made me

free from the law of sin and death. For what the law could not do, in that it was weak through the flesh, God sending his own Son in the likeness of sinful flesh, and for sin, condemned sin in the flesh: That the righteousness of the law might be fulfilled in us, who walk not after the flesh, but after the Spirit. For they that are after the flesh do mind the things of the flesh; but they that are after the Spirit the things of the Spirit. For to be carnally minded is death; but to be spiritually minded is life and peace. Because the carnal mind is enmity against God: for it is not subject to the law of God, neither indeed can be. So then they that are in the flesh cannot please God. But ye are not in the flesh, but in the Spirit, if so be that the Spirit of God dwell in you. Now if any man have not the Spirit of Christ, he is none of his. And if Christ be in you, the body is dead because of sin; but the Spirit is life because of righteousness. But if the Spirit of him that raised up Jesus from the dead dwell in you, he that raised up Christ from the dead shall also quicken your mortal bodies by his Spirit that dwelleth in you. Therefore, brethren, we are debtors, not to the flesh, to live after the flesh. For if ye live after the flesh, ye shall die: but if ye through the Spirit do mortify the deeds of the body, ye shall live. For as many as are led by the Spirit of God, they are the sons of God. For ye have not received the spirit of bondage again to fear; but ye have received the Spirit of adoption, whereby we cry, Abba, Father. The Spirit itself beareth witness with our spirit, that we are the children of God: And if children, then heirs; heirs of God, and joint-heirs with Christ; if so be that we suffer with him, that we may be also glorified together. For I reckon that the sufferings of this present time are not worthy to be compared with the glory which shall be revealed in us. For the earnest expectation of the creature waiteth for the manifestation of the sons of God. For the creature was made subject to vanity, not willingly, but by reason of him who hath subjected the same in hope, Because the creature itself also shall be delivered from the bondage of corruption into the glorious liberty of the children of God. For we know that the whole creation groaneth and travaileth in pain together until now. And not only they, but ourselves also, which have the firstfruits of the Spirit, even we ourselves groan within ourselves, waiting for the adoption, to wit, the redemption of our body. For we are saved by hope: but hope that is seen is not hope: for what a man seeth, why doth he yet hope for? But if we hope for that we see not, then do we with patience wait for it. Likewise the Spirit also helpeth our infirmities: for we know not what we should pray for as we ought: but the Spirit itself maketh intercession for us with groanings which cannot be uttered. And he that searcheth the hearts knoweth what is the mind of the Spirit, because he maketh intercession for the saints according to the will of God. And we know that all things work together for good to them that love God, to them who are the called according to his purpose. For whom he did foreknow, he also did predestinate to be conformed to the image of his Son, that he might be the firstborn among many brethren. Moreover whom he did predestinate, them he also called: and whom he called, them he also justified: and whom he justified, them he also glorified. What shall we then say to these things? If God be for us, who can be against us? He that spared not his own Son, but delivered him up for us all, how shall he not with him also freely give us all things? Who shall lay any thing to the charge of God's elect? It is God that justifieth. Who is he that condemneth? It is Christ that died, yea rather, that is risen again, who is even at the right hand of God, who also maketh intercession for us. Who shall separate us from the love of Christ?

shall tribulation, or distress, or persecution, or famine, or nakedness, or peril, or sword? As it is written, For thy sake we are killed all the day long; we are accounted as sheep for the slaughter. Nay, in all these things we are more than conquerors through him that loved us. For I am persuaded, that neither death, nor life, nor angels, nor principalities, nor powers, nor things present, nor things to come, Nor height, nor depth, nor any other creature, shall be able to separate us from the love of God, which is in Christ Jesus our Lord." (Romans 8:1-39 KJV)

You could not be separated from the voice of God even if you wanted to be! There is no escaping the Presence of God, just as the psalmist said, and, in the words of Paul referenced here we find that it is actually through creation that the glory of God is being revealed. The secret to being able to see God more clearly within the realm of physical, human flesh is to have a renewed mind of the Holy Spirit. Without faith, as the scriptures declare, it is impossible to please God. Without faith and without the renewed mind of the Spirit, too, it is impossible to hear God clearly and accurately. But when awakening comes and when the eyes of the understanding become enlightened, you, my fellow seeker, will both see and hear God in all the world around you.

CHAPTER SIX

"GOD IN 3-D"

An eternity before even the very Beginning, there existed the voice of God, the Word of God, and the Mind of God – and we existed there, also, in the heart of the Creator. Long before the words "Let there be" were ever uttered, there was a sense of knowing – a sense of intention so divine and so powerful that the force to enact creation was already present. Long before there was ever a physical world names Planet Earth and long before the physical, human form of man was ever formed and fashioned from the dust of the ground, even then there existed the voice of God. And there existed the powerful force of intention. To negate this would be to imply that God created haphazardly and without thought or planning – that He in some way just acted on a whim. No. There was careful planning. There was careful craftiness. There was intention, even then – long before even the very Beginning.

"In the beginning God created the heaven and the earth. And the earth was without form, and void; and darkness was upon the face of the deep. And the Spirit of God moved upon the face of the waters. And God said, Let there be light: and there was light. And God saw the light, that it was good: and God divided the light from the darkness. And God called the light Day, and the darkness he called Night. And the evening and the morning were the first day. And God said, Let there be a firmament in the midst of the

waters, and let it divide the waters from the waters. And God made the firmament, and divided the waters which were under the firmament from the waters which were above the firmament: and it was so. And God called the firmament Heaven. And the evening and the morning were the second day. And God said, Let the waters under the heaven be gathered together unto one place, and let the dry land appear: and it was so. And God called the dry land Earth; and the gathering together of the waters called he Seas: and God saw that it was good. And God said, Let the earth bring forth grass, the herb yielding seed, and the fruit tree yielding fruit after his kind, whose seed is in itself, upon the earth: and it was so. And the earth brought forth grass, and herb yielding seed after his kind, and the tree yielding fruit, whose seed was in itself, after his kind: and God saw that it was good. And the evening and the morning were the third day. And God said, Let *there be lights in the firmament of the heaven to divide the day from the night; and let them be for signs, and for seasons, and for days, and years: And let them be for lights in the firmament of the heaven to give light upon the earth: and it was so. And God made two great lights; the greater light to rule the day, and the lesser light to rule the night: he made the stars also. And God set them in the firmament of the heaven to give light upon the earth, And to rule over the day and over the night, and to divide the light from the darkness: and God saw that it was good. And the evening and the morning were the fourth day. And God said, Let the waters bring forth abundantly the moving creature that hath life, and fowl that may fly above the earth in the open firmament of heaven. And God created great whales, and every living creature that moveth, which the waters brought forth abundantly, after their kind, and every winged fowl after his kind: and*

God saw that it was good. And God blessed them, saying, Be fruitful, and multiply, and fill the waters in the seas, and let fowl multiply in the earth. And the evening and the morning were the fifth day. And God said, Let the earth bring forth the living creature after his kind, cattle, and creeping thing, and beast of the earth after his kind: and it was so. And God made the beast of the earth after his kind, and cattle after their kind, and every thing that creepeth upon the earth after his kind: and God saw that it was good. And God said, Let us make man in our image, after our likeness: and let them have dominion over the fish of the sea, and over the fowl of the air, and over the cattle, and over all the earth, and over every creeping thing that creepeth upon the earth. So God created man in his own image, in the image of God created he him; male and female created he them. And God blessed them, and God said unto them, Be fruitful, and multiply, and replenish the earth, *and subdue it: and have dominion over the fish of the sea, and over the fowl of the air, and over every living thing that moveth upon the earth. And God said, Behold, I have given you every herb bearing seed, which is upon the face of all the earth, and every tree, in the which is the fruit of a tree yielding seed; to you it shall be for meat. And to every beast of the earth, and to every fowl of the air, and to every thing that creepeth upon the earth, wherein there is life, I have given every green herb for meat: and it was so. And God saw every thing that he had made, and, behold, it was very good. And the evening and the morning were the sixth day."* (Genesis 1:1-31 KJV)

God not only spoke Creation into existence, infusing it with His very own Word, but in doing so God literally infused Creation with His very own self and His very own divine essence. The mystics of various other world religions have taught that God did not only create Creation but that, to some degree, God literally became Creation. Though the concept might seem absurd at first glance, we find, to some certain degree, this principle even in the account of Creation when the Creator forms man from the dust of the ground and breathes into him the Breath of Life, causing man to become a living, breathing soul. Could it be that the very nature of God has, in fact, been three-dimensional all along? Could it be that God, in fact, has taken on human form much longer than religions seek to suggest?

Man was the crowning jewel of all Creation, as the Creator breathed into man His very own essence – the Breath of Life. And it was in that instant that even the newly created man became an extension of God within the realm of Earth. The original term for "soul" within the original language of the text is "anima," from which is derived the more modern concept of "animation" or movement." Imagine that for a moment. Even the movement of man was caused by the very breathe of God! It's truly no wonder now, is it, that the scriptures make it plain that it is in Him that we live and breathe and move and have our very being. Suffice it to say, all of Creation is but an extension of the essence of the Creator – and so are you. Knowing this, how much more should we have confidence knowing that hearing the voice of God is our divine birthright? It's not only natural to hear the voice of God and to experience God in all aspects of Creation, but to not do so is what's truly unnatural. It's unnatural for you to feel disconnected. It's unnatural for you to have to fight and war against yourself within your own natural mind, questioning and wondering with uncertainty, not knowing if you're hearing from God. There is nothing more natural than communication with Heaven!

In an instant, as man became infused with the very Breathe of Life and became a living, breathing soul, suddenly, the supernatural became natural and the heavenly became worldly. The very nature of God became infused into three-dimensional space and time and the reality of Earth became a mere extension of Heaven. The newly formed Creation was so "good," in fact, that even the Creator marveled at His handiwork. Today, though, there seems to so often be forgetfulness of this, where religion is concerned. Today, mankind has been led to erroneously believe that Heaven is reserved only for some future place or time and that to access Heaven means that we must first abandon our humanity and everything that makes us who we are while we're here residing upon Planet Earth. My friend and fellow seeker, such is simply not the case nor has it ever been.

It's time to begin to see God in a much more three-dimensional way than ever before. When you do, I assure you that you will never again question whether or not you hear the voice of God but you will, instead, begin to recognize that the Holy Spirit is always, always speaking. Remember, as the early church fathers shared, God has many, many unique ways of drawing us to Himself. You may ask, "Even in a very natural world?" Absolutely so. In fact, the glory of God which resided within the realm of Heaven was made so apparently clear in Creation that even Jesus himself remarked about such glory before going to the crucifixion, stating that even the glory which resided in the Beginning has been given to men and women. The only separation has always, always existed solely within the mind of man and never even for one instant within the heart or the mind of God.

Yes, a very real "fall" did take place; however the fall was always within the mind of man, as the natural mind developed a consciousness of sin after tasting of the tree of the *knowledge* of good and evil. Thankfully, though, because of the Holy Spirit and through communion with God, humanity is daily being given an opportunity to awaken to a greater, better understanding of the things of God – always being given the opportunity to come to the place of the renewed mind. Spiritual things can only be discerned and recognized through the eyes of the Spirit, and it is for this cause that the mind must be renewed. In order for the natural mind to be renewed, though, it must first be stretched beyond its old way of thinking. It must sometimes even be offended in order to become changed and renewed.

Let's face it; it offends the religious mind to hear that God uses even daily life within the natural world to speak to us. Religion would must rather seek to dominate the monopoly on who hears the voice of God and on how God speaks. Is it truly any wonder why the scriptures declare that the natural religious mind is the very enemy of God? To see and to better hear, though, the mind must be renewed. To begin to see God in all Creation around you demands that you shift your perspective from the place of judgment to the place of love and acceptance. I've said for years and have seen confirmed more and more throughout years of ministry that absolutely nothing deafens the senses and deafens our spiritual ears to the voice of God quite like judgment. If you think about it, religion, by its very definition, is a form of judgment – a judgment of others and also, to possibly an even greater extent, a judgment of our own selves.

If you truly desire to hear God and to see God in operation all around you, begin by removing judgment. Begin by removing the mindset that says "That's not God" or "Surely God wouldn't speak that way." Has it ever occurred to you that possibly, as well-intentioned as you've been in your own religious zeal and fervor, you've missed the forest for the trees, as the old analogy goes? The voice of God is expansive. It is transcendent. And it is, above all, permeating and piercing. It permeates deeply as the scriptures declare, revealing motives and intentions and even the thoughts we think. There's a lot to be said of even the very thoughts we think, and I'll share more on that soon. However, suffice it to say, for now, that the voice of God speaks deeply within us to the point that even the inner, deeper thoughts we think are in many ways aspects of the voice of God.

"Let us therefore fear, lest, a promise being left us of entering into his rest, any of you should seem to come short of it. For unto us was the gospel preached, as well as unto them: but the word preached did not profit them, not being mixed with faith in them that heard it. For we which have believed do enter into rest, as he said, As I have sworn in my wrath, if they shall enter into my rest: although the works were finished from the foundation of the world. For he spake in a certain place of the seventh day on this wise, And God did rest the seventh day from all his works. And in this place again, If they shall enter into my rest. Seeing therefore it remaineth that some must enter therein, and they to whom it was first preached entered not in because of unbelief: Again, he limiteth a certain day, saying in David, To day, after so long a time; as it is said, To day if ye will hear his voice, harden not your hearts. For if Jesus had given them rest, then would he not

afterward have spoken of another day. There remaineth therefore a rest to the people of God. For he that is entered into his rest, he also hath ceased from his own works, as God did from his. Let us labour therefore to enter into that rest, lest any man fall after the same example of unbelief. For the word of God is quick, and powerful, and sharper than any twoedged sword, piercing even to the dividing asunder of soul and spirit, and of the joints and marrow, and is a discerner of the thoughts and intents of the heart. Neither is there any creature that is not manifest in his sight: but all things are naked and opened unto the eyes of him with whom we have to do. Seeing then that we have a great high priest, that is passed into the heavens, Jesus the Son of God, let us hold fast our profession. For we have not an high priest which cannot be touched with the feeling of our infirmities; but was in all points tempted like as we are, yet without sin. Let us therefore come boldly unto the throne of grace, that we may obtain mercy, and find grace to help in time of need." (Hebrews 4:1-16 KJV)

The writer of the Book of Hebrews makes mention of the boldness – the confidence – that always comes to those who hear the Word of the LORD. Doubt is erased and gives way to confidence when the sense of knowing replaces mere religious wishing and thinking. And when it does, we can begin to see the things of God all around us, in a more three-dimensional way. We can begin to see that God has always been speaking not only to Creation but also through Creation. There has never been a time in which Creation hasn't been calling out to us, reminding us of the things of the Spirit. Truly, Heaven has invaded the realm of Earth – that is, for those who can choose to see it.

CHAPTER SEVEN

INTENTIONAL ANSWERS

Knowing now that the realm of heaven has permeated all of Earth and all of your daily life and that the voice of God is ever-present and always in existence within you, all around you, and, indeed, through you, it's time to begin to become much more proactive and much more intentional where the voice of God is concerned within your life. When I hear countless passionate, well-intentioned seekers express to me their desire to hear the prophetic voice of God much more clearly, I often reply, "How much do you want it?" The question truly must be asked. After all, it was Jesus who offered the heavenly, blessed assurance that those who hunger and thirst shall be filled. And so, now, I would ask you, personally, when it comes to hearing the voice of God within your life and when it comes to being able to more correctly discern the inner voice within and awakening your own prophetic gift, how much do you truly want it?

Your thoughts matter. Your feelings matter. And, as you will soon realize all the more, your intention matters – especially where hearing the voice of God is concerned. What do you intend to do to develop your sensitivity to the Holy Spirit? What do you plan to do to better hear the voice of God within your own life? Now that you have a better more comprehensive knowledge of the realm of Heaven being all around you and now that you're able to more clearly see just how tied you are to the Word of

God – realizing that you couldn't even be separated from it even if you tried to be – what are you going to begin to do within your own life each day to sharpen your spiritual sight and open your spiritual ears all the more?

Now that you know the Kingdom is in operation all around you, always, at all times, speaking to you through daily life, what are you, as the seeker to do with this revelation? Are we, as believers, to simply sit idly by and believe that we already have it all, or is there actually a very real role that we've been given to play? As religion seems to suggest, is the voice of God simply dropped into our laps from on high, or is there very real work to be done if we are to ever correctly discern the voice of God within the physical, natural world? The answers may surprise you. As you will see, yes, the Kingdom is in full operation; however, you and I, as seekers of God, have always had a tremendous responsibility. Although the Word is within you and around you and working through you, it's going to be up to you to both see and to hear God in your own daily life.

In Pauls' instructions to young Timothy, he admonishes the young believer to do the work of "dividing" the Word within his life, detailing to Timothy as well as to the early church that for the Word to be correctly received, it must be correctly discerned. This in itself implies a certain sense of work and responsibility on the part of the believer. For you, my fellow seeker, it's not going to be enough to simply believe that God is speaking to you throughout your daily life, in the world around you; you're going to have to begin to become more open in seeking out the voice of God in life and become more active in actually learning to look for the many ways in which God speaks. Revelation doesn't come simply through impartation;

revelation comes through seeking – by asking, by seeking, and by knocking. You're not going to suddenly receive the answers you seek simply by hearing a teaching or by standing in a prayer line at some revival service. Instead, you're going to have to begin to correctly divide the world within your own life and realize that God is speaking to you in three-dimensional ways all hours of the day and night.

"Thou therefore, my son, be strong in the grace that is in Christ Jesus. And the things that thou hast heard of me among many witnesses, the same commit thou to faithful men, who shall be able to teach others also. Thou therefore endure hardness, as a good soldier of Jesus Christ. No man that warreth entangleth himself with the affairs of this life; that he may please him who hath chosen him to be a soldier. And if a man also strive for masteries, yet is he not crowned, except he strive lawfully. The

husbandman that laboureth must be first partaker of the fruits. Consider what I say; and the Lord give thee understanding in all things. Remember that Jesus Christ of the seed of David was raised from the dead according to my gospel: Wherein I suffer trouble, as an evil doer, even unto bonds; but the word of God is not bound. Therefore I endure all things for the elect's sakes, that they may also obtain the salvation which is in Christ Jesus with eternal glory. It is a faithful saying: For if we be dead with him, we shall also live with him: If we suffer, we shall also reign with him: if we deny him, he also will deny us: If we believe not, yet he abideth faithful: he cannot deny himself. Of these things put them in remembrance, charging them before the Lord that they strive not about words to no profit, but to the subverting of the hearers. Study to shew thyself approved unto God, a workman that needeth not to be ashamed, rightly dividing the word of truth. But shun profane and vain babblings: for they will increase unto more ungodliness. And their word will eat as doth a canker: of whom is Hymenaeus and Philetus; Who concerning the truth have erred, saying that the resurrection is past already; and overthrow the faith of some. Nevertheless the foundation of God standeth sure, having this seal, The Lord knoweth them that are his. And, let every one that nameth the name of Christ depart from iniquity. But in a great house there are not only vessels of gold and of silver, but also of wood and of earth; and some to honour, and some to dishonour. If a man therefore purge himself from these, he shall be a vessel unto honour, sanctified, and meet for the master's use, and prepared unto every good work. Flee also youthful lusts: but follow righteousness, faith, charity, peace, with them that call on the Lord out of a pure heart. But foolish and unlearned questions avoid, knowing that they do gender strifes. And the servant of the Lord must not strive; but be gentle unto all men, apt to teach, patient, In meekness instructing those that oppose themselves; if God peradventure will give them repentance to the acknowledging of the truth; And that they may recover themselves out of the snare of the devil, who are taken captive by him at his will." (2 Timothy 2:1-26 KJV)

Notice, if you will, that within Paul's instruction to Timothy, he outlines very detailed and very practical steps for how to better align with the Word of God. Paul even states emphatically that we must be "partakers" of the Word in daily life. What many sincere and well-intentioned believers often miss, though, is that Paul wasn't speaking to Timothy regarding the study of books and ancient texts alone. No. In fact, the text that would come to be recognized as the scriptures that we now know would not come into existence until nearly three centuries later.

At the time of Paul's admonishment to Timothy, there were the words of the prophets, the Law of Moses, and the gift of prophecy – and nothing else. When Paul addressed Timothy and the early church, there was no Holy Bible as we now know it. There was only the inspiration of the Holy Spirit coming into the lives of men and women. After all, even the text of the ancient scriptures notes that the scriptures came by inspiration of God. However, the text had not been formally canonized at the time. And so, when Paul spoke of rightly "dividing" the Word of Truth, what then was he actually speaking of?

To better understand the role of the prophetic gift and to better and more clearly discern the voice of God within daily life, it's important to begin to better understand the true meaning of "The Word." Today, in this more modern time of ours, the idea of "The Word" conjures many different and varying images and beliefs. To even hear the term "The Word," for most, the mind begins to conjure images of a leather-bound book. Remember, though, in the first century church, the Bible did not exist yet. When the early church spoke of the Word, they were speaking of something much, much more transcendent than mere books and writings; they were speaking, instead, of a very real inner gift. They were peaking of "inspiration."

If we take notice of the term "inspiration," we find that the term literally is derived from two words: "in" and "spirit." And so, when we speak of inspiration what we are actually referring to is being "in the Spirit." To be inspired, in fact, means to align yourself with the things of the Spirit. The early church and those early believers recognized in an exciting and revelatory way that the inner inspiration we feel – the inner drive – is actually the Word of God in operation within us. They recognized the principle that to be led by the Spirit is actually to be *inspired* by the Spirit. Does this not change how many view the concept of "The Word?" "The Word," you see, has never been relegated or confined to a leather-bound book. It has always, always been something much more innate – much more transcendent. When Paul spoke to Timothy about how to better, more accurately "divide" the Word, what he was in fact saying was, "Live an inspired life!"

Regardless of your beliefs and regardless of your theology, all your life you've been driven from within. You've possessed dreams and desires that could only be described as inescapable. Even now, as you read these words, your soul is crying out. The soul, consisting of the mind, the will, and the emotions, has always been the inner compass of your life, even though you may not have always recognized it. Knowing this, then, it's truly no exaggeration to state that your thoughts matter, your desires matter, and, yes, even your wants matter within the Kingdom of Heaven. Do you truly want to know what God is saying to you? Begin by recognizing what truly inspires you! To hear the voice of the Holy Spirit within your own life, begin to recognize more fully what is inspiring you within your life. *That* is the Word within you. *That* is the Word made flesh.

One of the most shocking, most telling examples of this is found in Paul's epistle to the early church at Rome, when he details "The Word" in such a transcendent way, stating that we have power in what we believe. *"But what saith it? The word is nigh thee, even in thy mouth, and in thy heart: that is, the word of faith, which we preach; That if thou shalt confess with thy mouth the Lord Jesus, and shalt believe in thine heart that God hath raised him from the dead, thou shalt be saved. For with the heart man believeth unto righteousness; and with the mouth confession is made unto salvation." Romans 10:8-10 KJV)* For centuries we've heard within the Body of Christ the importance of making a confession unto salvation; however, very rarely has there ever been an emphasis placed upon the first portion of the passage. Consider it for a moment: "The Word is nigh thee."

What inspires you each day? What drives you each day? What captures your attention each day and leads you from within? What is the dream that seems so inescapable for you? The dream that no matter what you just can't seem to shake? What are you passionate about? What are the passions that lead you all throughout the day and even into the night, haunting your dreams? That is the voice of God within you. And if you're ever going to truly discern the Word of God within your life – the voice of God, that is – you're going to have to begin to rightly "divide" yourself.

The Book of James even makes mention of this, noting that for the Word to actually work, work must be done within. *"James, a servant of God and of the Lord Jesus Christ, to the twelve tribes which are scattered abroad, greeting. My brethren, count it all joy when ye fall into divers temptations; Knowing this, that the trying of your faith worketh patience. But let patience have her perfect work, that ye may be perfect and entire, wanting nothing. If any of you lack wisdom, let him ask of God, that giveth to all men liberally, and upbraideth not; and it shall be given him. But let him ask in faith, nothing wavering. For he that wavereth is like a wave of the sea driven with the wind and tossed. For let not that man think that he shall receive any thing of the Lord. A double minded man is unstable in all his ways. Let the brother of low degree rejoice in that he is exalted: But the rich, in that he is made low: because as the flower of the grass he shall pass away. For the sun is no sooner risen with a burning heat, but it withereth the grass, and the flower thereof falleth, and the grace of the fashion of it perisheth: so also shall the rich man fade away in his ways. Blessed is the man that endureth temptation: for when he is tried, he shall receive the crown of life, which the Lord hath promised to them that love him. Let no man say when he is tempted, I am tempted of God: for God cannot be tempted with evil, neither tempteth he any man: But every man is tempted, when he is drawn away of his own lust, and enticed. Then when lust hath conceived, it bringeth forth sin: and sin, when it is finished, bringeth forth death. Do not err, my beloved brethren. Every good gift and every perfect gift is from above, and cometh down from the Father of lights, with whom is no variableness, neither shadow of* turning. Of his own will begat he us with the word of truth, that we should be a kind of firstfruits of his creatures. Wherefore, my beloved brethren, let every man be swift to hear, slow to speak, slow to wrath: For the wrath of man worketh not the righteousness of God. Wherefore lay apart all filthiness and superfluity of naughtiness, and receive with meekness the engrafted word, which is able to save your souls. But be ye doers of the word, and not hearers only, deceiving your own selves. For if any be a hearer of the word, and not a doer, he is like unto a man beholding his natural face in a glass: For he beholdeth himself, and goeth his way, and straightway forgetteth what manner of man he was. But whoso looketh into the perfect law of liberty, and continueth therein, he being not a forgetful hearer, but a doer of the work, this man shall be blessed in his deed. If any man among you seem to be religious, and bridleth not his tongue, but *deceiveth his own heart, this man's religion is vain. Pure religion and undefiled before God and the Father is this, To visit the fatherless and widows in their affliction, and to keep himself unspotted from the world." (James 1:1-27 KJV)*

The writer of the Book of James emphasizes continuously within the text the vast importance of not only hearing the Word but actually doing the Word – actively working out the Word in daily, physical life. But how, exactly does one go about being a "doer" of the Word? Quite simply put, they surrender to the inner drive of the inspiration within them. In the writing of the Book of James, we find a very real parallel between hearing and doing – a parallel so very real it's unmistakable. Do you truly desire to hear the Word of God? If so, then begin to surrender to the inner drive of the inspiration within you. Do you desire to hear God more clearly and much more accurately than ever before? If so then begin to recognize what's been driving you all along. If you truly desire to correctly, rightly "divide" the Word of Truth, begin by delving more deeply into your own self. After all, as Jesus said, that's where the Kingdom truly is. It always has been. It always will be.

"But be ye doers of the word, and not hearers only, deceiving your own selves. For if any be a hearer of the word, and not a doer, he is like unto a man beholding his natural face in a glass: For he beholdeth himself, and goeth his way, and straightway forgetteth what manner of man he was. But whoso looketh into the perfect law of liberty, and continueth therein, he being not a forgetful hearer, but a doer of the work, this man shall be blessed in his deed." It's not enough to simply hear the voice of God – to simply know what drives you and what inspires you. You're going to have to begin to put it into

action. You're going to have to begin to do it. The abundant life comes only in doing.

CHAPTER EIGHT

THE WORD WITHIN

When you stop fighting against yourself and cease from condemning yourself, you'll begin to hear the inner voice of God much more clearly. And, surprisingly, you'll then even begin to hear the voice of God all around you, as well. When the noise of inner war ceases, there will come the voice of God in the silence within. To end the constantt, raging war within, though, requires being able to recognize that not only are you loved by God but that God has always desired communion with you. There is no separation in love. There is no judgment in love. There is no fear. For as the scriptures remind us, perfect love casts out fear.

It's time to begin to think and to live more positively. Nothing deafens the spiritual senses quite like doubt and unbelief. Rather than judging yourself and your situation, begin, instead, to realize that God is speaking to you and leading you even in the midst of some of your most confusing situations. What I've found within my own life and see day after day throughout my work in ministry is that the moment you begin to shift your perspective of yourself and gain a greater level of confidence, the more you'll begin to know the voice of God within your life and the more you, in turn, even begin to find the answers to those most burning, most pressing questions. What if you could begin to realize that all of the answers you seek are simply waiting to be discovered – that they are simply waiting for you to uncover them? Within the Kingdom of Heaven, this is entirely the case.

When Jesus spoke of the importance of asking, seeking, and knocking, he was speaking emphatically about the power of discovery. In fact, even more so, he was referring to a very real journey of faith – the journey of life. Personally, I refuse to believe that life is meant to always be filled with struggle and with hardship. More times than not, if we were to be honest with ourselves, we would admit that so often the greatest struggles and the greatest hardships of life have come upon us the moment that we began to doubt ourselves. Within the Kingdom of Heaven and within all matters of life, hasn't this always been the case? Something very deadly begins to happen when doubt comes and when we begin to question ourselves. Confidence leave and becomes replaced, instead, with uncertainty. And before long, when doubt and insecurity have taken root, we find ourselves in a state of complacency, viewing ourselves as victims of life rather than victors within the Kingdom. Hear me when I say to you that the way in which you hear the voice of God is directly tied to what you choose to believe about your own self.

It's a proven fact, contrary to the lies of organized religion, that it's not enough to simply believe in the power of God; you must also believe in the power residing within your very own self. That isn't some humanist approach to the Gospel, as some erroneously suggest. That is the Gospel! After all, Jesus himself declared that not only will we be given what we believe but that we will be given exactly what we believe. And so, even now as you read these words, if you're feeling dissatisfied and uncertain, chances are, somewhere along the way, not only did stop believing in the reality of a three-dimensional God but you also stopped believing in yourself. It's all too common, really. The moment that you begin to doubt yourself, the moment you begin to feel powerless and helpless. But we are not as those who have no hope, thankfully.

Not only is it important that you begin to trust yourself more, but this trust and belief in yourself is essential – crucial, even – where the abundant life is concerned. So often I hear many sincere believers express to me, "Jeremy, I believe in God, but I have no confidence in myself." Often this damnable belief comes from religious indoctrination, as we're told time after time that nothing good exists within us. Chances are you've even heard it in this way: "The only thing good about me is God." It sounds humble doesn't it? Well, it isn't. Not even hardly. False humility is nothing more than the lies of religion, and it's keeping you from not only the abundant life you've been promised but it's also keeping you from living the life of your dreams. If you don't believe in yourself then the fact of the matter is that you don't truly believe in God the way that you claim. After all, you are formed in His image and in His likeness – His very essence causing you to move and to act and to experience life within the physical world. It simply cannot be overstated that what you believe even about God is a direct reflection of what you choose to believe about your very own self.

"As He is, so are we," as the scriptures declare. You are the manifested Presence of God within this realm of Earth, called to manifest the Kingdom of God within three-dimensional space and time. Right now, all of Creation around you is expressing the glory of God and manifesting the Kingdom. When you question yourself and begin to doubt your ability to hear God clearly, rather than co-creating an abundant life with God, you're resigning yourself to the role of spectator. Because of religion, day after day, countless sincere believers fail to enact their God-given dreams and as a result continue to live lives of struggle and hardship, continuing to say, "I don't know what to do," even when the answers exist within them the entire time. It's time to hear God by becoming much more confident even in your own self.

If you find yourself reading these words and feeling so dissatisfied with the life you're now living, has it occurred to you that the very feeling of dissatisfaction is also Heaven's way of getting your attention and an attempt to remind you that you need to make a change in your own beliefs and action? When you know better, you begin to do better. Most often, the reason believers and sincere seekers of God never truly live out their potential is because they never truly understand that it is up to them to do so. God isn't going to simply impart unto you the abundant life. Those God-given dreams of yours aren't going to suddenly, miraculously come to pass. Your dream life will not suddenly, magically become imparted unto you. The abundant life is not a matter of luck. The abundant life is a matter of action!

So often, when teaching the gift of prophecy to my students and clients around the world, I like to use the early church as an example. After all, if the church is ever to truly experience a greater measure of the miraculous and the supernatural, it must return to the very Beginning of it all. There was a reason, you see, why such miraculous power existed within the early church, and the reason wasn't because of some select dispensation or anointing that existed only for them. The reason was because there was a confidence that existed that seems all too nonexistent in the modern church. There was boldness then. There was an assurance that can only come from knowing – not mere believing.

Think of this for a moment. Ponder it. Have you ever taken the time to consider that the faith we have today would not even exist were it not for men and women of old, in boldness and in confidence, hearing and then more importantly acting on the Word of God? If you study the Book of Acts, you find something truly remarkable concerning the voice of God. The apostles seemed to know exactly what to do, what to say, where to go, when to leave, and even who they would meet once they arrived! Today, there are many so-called believers who spend years praying about whether they should ask someone out on a first date! That's not faith, my friend; it's fear. And absolutely nothing will ever hinder you from living out the abundant life of your dreams quite like the fear that comes from not believing in yourself. Today, I want to encourage you to begin to get your confidence back again.

Yes, the voice of God exists all around you – in the thunder and in the lightning even. However, there is still much to be said about the importance of recognizing the still, small voice of God within you. In the stillness, the answers come. To put it more accurately, though, in the stillness the answers will become uncovered and revealed because the answers are already in existence within you in the first place. Truth is expansive – it grows and begins to emerge until it cannot be denied any longer. If there are questions you seek today, regarding, well, anything and everything, you need only to look within your own self. After all, that is where the realm of the Kingdom truly lies. The early church acted in boldness and in confidence without fear. Today, because of religious indoctrination, there is talk of such things as the "perfect" and the "permissive" will of God. But how often have such erroneous things kept you from acting? Do you want to be sure you're haring God clearly and accurately? Begin by making a move! Begin by taking a step of faith!

"And Ahab told Jezebel all that Elijah had done, and withal how he had slain all the prophets with the sword. Then Jezebel sent a messenger unto Elijah, saying, So let the gods do to me, and more also, if I make not thy life as the life of one of them by to morrow about this time. And when he saw that, he arose, and went for his life, and came to Beersheba, which belongeth to Judah, and left his servant there. But he himself went a day's journey into the wilderness, and came and sat down under a juniper tree: and he requested for himself that

he might die; and said, It is enough; now, O Lord, take away my life; for I am not better than my fathers. And as he lay and slept under a juniper tree, behold, then an angel touched him, and said unto him, Arise and eat. And he looked, and, behold, there was a cake baken on the coals, and a cruse of water at his head. And he did eat and drink, and laid him down again. And the angel of the Lord came again the second time, and touched him, and said, Arise and eat; because the journey is too great for thee. And he arose, and did eat and drink, and went in the strength of that meat forty days and forty nights unto Horeb the mount of God. And he came thither unto a cave, and lodged there; and, behold, the word of the Lord came to him, and he said unto him, What doest thou here, Elijah? And he said, I have been very jealous for the Lord God of hosts: for the children of Israel have forsaken thy covenant, thrown down thine altars, and slain thy prophets with the sword; and I, even I only, am left; and they seek my life, to take it away. And he said, Go forth, and stand upon the mount before the Lord. And, behold, the Lord passed by, and a great and strong wind rent the mountains, and brake in pieces the rocks before the Lord; but the Lord was not in the wind: and after the wind an earthquake; but the Lord was not in the earthquake: And after the earthquake a fire; but the Lord was not in the fire: and after the fire a still small voice. And it was so, when Elijah heard it, that he wrapped his face in his mantle, and went out, and stood in the entering in of the cave. And, behold, there came a voice unto him, and said, What doest thou here, Elijah? And he said, I have been very jealous for the Lord God of hosts: because the children of Israel have forsaken thy covenant, thrown down thine altars, and slain thy prophets with the sword; and I, even I only, am left; and they seek my life, to take it away. And the Lord said unto him,

Go, return on thy way to the wilderness of Damascus: and when thou comest, anoint Hazael to be king over Syria: And Jehu the son of Nimshi shalt thou anoint to be king over Israel: and Elisha the son of Shaphat of Abelmeholah shalt thou anoint to be prophet in thy room. And it shall come to pass, that him that escapeth the sword of Hazael shall Jehu slay: and him that escapeth from the sword of Jehu shall Elisha slay. Yet I have left me seven thousand in Israel, all the knees which have not bowed unto Baal, and every mouth which hath not kissed him. So he departed thence, and found Elisha the son of Shaphat, who was plowing with twelve yoke of oxen before him, and he with the twelfth: and Elijah passed by him, and cast his mantle upon him. And he left the oxen, and ran after Elijah, and said, Let me, I pray thee, kiss my father and my mother, and then I will follow thee. And he said unto him, Go back again: for what have I done to thee? And he returned back from him, and took a yoke of oxen, and slew them, and boiled their flesh with the instruments of the oxen, and gave unto the people, and they did eat. Then he arose, and went after Elijah, and ministered unto him." (1 Kings 19:1-21 KJV)

There's always a direct correlation between what you're hearing and what you're doing. How often throughout the centuries has the above referenced passage of text been used to depict the importance of hearing the still, small voice? We've heard it time and time again – that God is speaking to us in still, small ways. Well, although it's true, there is much to be said about movement and action. So much emphasis has been placed upon the importance of the still, small voice that so often religion seems to miss the actual message that was delivered. When the still, small voice came, it asked a question: "What are you doing?" Oh, how I pray that you would receive this revelation. My fellow believers, I promise you that if you will begin to finally act on what you know to do you will begin to hear the voice of God all the more in other areas of your life. You cannot truly experience the realm of God within your life until you begin to act on what you're already being led to do! Do you feel confused or uncertain concerning what God would have you to do? Well, what are you doing?

One of the most telling confirmations of this principle is found within the Book of Acts in possibly the most subtle of passages – a passage all too often casually disregarded. The passage is in Acts 15:28, text that outlines certain standards of living for the early, infantile church. *"For it seemed good to the Holy Ghost, and to us, to lay upon you no greater burden than these necessary things; That ye abstain from meats offered to idols, and from blood, and from things strangled, and from fornication: from which if ye keep yourselves, ye shall do well. Fare ye well." (Acts 15:28-29 KJV)* And here, within the opening words of the passage we find what is possibly the singular greatest cause for the confidence that existed within the early church: agreement. Not only did decision making seem good to the Holy Ghost, but it seemed good to the early apostles.

For most of your life, where the voice of God is concerned, you've so often found yourself wondering, asking, "Does this decision seem good to God?" "Will Heaven be pleased with this decision?" "If I begin the new business, will God be pleased?" "If I begin the new relationship, will it seem good to God?" "If I decide to go back to school to continue my education, will it seem good to God?" My friend, the question is, "Does it seem good to you?"

Something truly heavenly begins to happen when action and when doing is paired with your ability to hear the voice of God within you. Agreement with Heaven becomes activated all the more and the realm of possibilities becomes altogether infinite and limitless! In closing, I would ask, what seems good to you? As you go throughout your day being led by the Holy Spirit, feeling the inner drive – the inner inspiration of God within you – what seems good to you? It's time to begin to ask yourself this all-important question. And it's time to act.

Right now, even as you read these words, there are cemeteries now filled with the bodies of those who, in their lives, were sincere and well-intentioned believers – believers who felt the inner inspiration of God leading them each day. Unlike some, though, these believers failed to act. They waited. They prayed. They longed for countless confirmation after confirmation.

And then, many of them died without ever having fulfilled their God-given dreams. Were they loved by God? Of course. Are they now within the realm of Heaven? Of course. However, what they failed to recognize within their earthly lives is that Heaven becomes all the more real even within the realm of Earth when the decision is made to act.

CHAPTER NINE

THE WORD EXTERNAL

I'll never forget flying back from a conference in Anaheim not that long ago. I had been scheduled to be a featured presenter at a ministry event, teaching prophecy. It was an extraordinary week filled with miracles and activations of healing and impartation. The glory of God was so present – so tangible and so real and palpable. I always enjoy ministering to audiences and I count it a blessing and a privilege to reach the world with the Gospel. In that season of my life, though, it was a very stressful time. There was so much to do. Anyone who tells you that ministry is easy doesn't truly minister. It takes work to balance schedules, to travel, and to pour your heart into the lives of other people. In that season of my life, Identity Network was in a time of expansion and rapid growth, and I was prayerfully considering signing a new publishing deal for what would have been, at the time my thirtieth book. I was grateful. But I was personally exhausted.

Even traveling to the airport seemed stressful, as I prepared to board the flight. As I sat in traffic, feeling what seemed to be the weight of the world upon my shoulders, it became all too clear that reality had begun to sink in. Yes, the glory was still very real within me, but I knew that upon returning home I would have some very important decisions to make concerning the future of Identity Network. Would I publish more books? Would I continue to write?

Would I travel even more in the coming year? There were so many questions it was unbearable. Over the weekend, it seemed the Word had come so quickly and so effortlessly into the lives of those in attendance. One by one seekers seemed to receive prophetically the insight they had longed for. I have to admit, though, that day I was in need of some direction of my own. I even missed my flight back after being delayed in traffic!

Once I was able to board the plane, I found myself seated next to a man name Bill. After the morning I'd had I honestly didn't feel like having conversation, but I smiled and introduced myself. He asked about my travels and I replied, simply, "I've been traveling on business." Unbeknownst to me, though, Bill was actually something of a conversationalist. He continued to talk – and talk and talk. I listened as politely as possible, as my mind continued to race. He shared stories of his family and his job. I continued to listen. And then, seemingly out of the blue, Bill said something to me that struck me to my core – something that I'll never forget. Bill said, with a laugh, "It's funny all the ways God reminds us that we're right where we're supposed to be." Those words struck me to the core of my being. I knew those words to be true. In that moment, though, I had received the reminder that I had needed. I looked out the window of the plane in that moment to see a beautiful rainbow – a reminder of God's promises.

We call them "signs" – those moments in which it seems the Universe is seeking to get our attention. The truth of the matter though is that they aren't truly signs as much as they are universal synchronicities – effects of divine, heavenly alignment. If I had taken an earlier flight and hadn't been delayed, I would have never met Bill. I would have never been given the encouraging word I had needed. I would have missed the view of the beautiful rainbow. As I traveled back, in that moment, I felt an overwhelming, heavenly peace of mind – a peace that I'd needed. I share this very real, very personal story with you to say, quite simply, not only is God speaking to you internally but God is also speaking to you externally, as well, through other people and, yes, shockingly, even through nature. As the ancient writers have said, God truly does have many ways of drawing you to himself – even when it may not always seem like it.

I have a dear friend who once found himself battling depression after the loss of his career. He felt so alone in the world after having experienced what could only be described as a devastating loss in a season of overwhelming setback within his life. He needed a getaway as a way to decompress and to clear his mind. He wanted to get as far as humanly possible from everything and everyone around him. When he found himself walking the crowded, busy streets of a city in which he'd never been, he found himself thinking, wondering, "Where am I even going in life?" He just continued to walk the crowded, busy streets aimlessly. He didn't even new where he was going or what he was looking for or hoping to find. When the road forked and he found himself at a crossroad, he even considered flipping a coin just to decide which road to take. Ultimately he chose the road that led to the waterfront. He had hoped to clear his mind. And then, shockingly, to his amazement and to his surprise, he saw a childhood friend standing by the water's edge, fishing! No one else was around! It seemed the childhood friend had needed a getaway for himself as well!

There are no accidents. There are no coincidences – not in this life or in the next. And especially not in the Kingdom of Heaven. It's time to remove even the term "coincidental" from your vocabulary once and for all. Hear me when I say to you that not only is everything happening within you just as it should but that, also, everything is happening around you just as it should as well. What are the chances that in a foreign city literally thousands of miles away, wondering aimlessly through crowded busy streets, a man would just happen upon a childhood friend? Statistically, it's highly improbable to say the very least. But in that moment, the synchronicity was exactly what was needed, as all of Heaven aligned with all of Earth to create what could have only been described as a "sign."

The scriptures make it plain that signs will always follow them that believe. Today, in this more modern world of Christendom, we so often think of signs as the otherworldly and the miraculous. We think of the many notable extraordinary feats outlined in the sixteenth chapter of the Gospel according to Mark – speaking in tongues, casting out devils and healing the sick. However, if you would be sensitive to the leading of the Holy Spirit, being more present in all matters of daily life, you'll be shocked to realize that signs are always, always happening all around you all throughout the day and even in the night, even while you sleep. Yes, God still speaks even in the dream-state. And, yes, prophetic insight still comes to those who believe even when they least expect it. It's time to rethink "signs" in a more present way than ever before.

Chances are when you went to the market for groceries, the voice of God was the very last thing on your mind. In fact, I would dare to make the claim that your trip to the market probably didn't feel very spiritual at all. But what if God was attempting to speak to you through the man in line at the register? Or the elderly woman you passed while you were walking back to your car? I would ask, if so, would you have noticed? Would you have gotten the message? You see, all too often we think of the voice of God as being the still, small inner voice or even the otherworldly, cataclysmic, Earth-shattering moments of divine intervention. I would humbly ask, though, what if the voice of God came in the form of a smile from the random stranger you passed on the street? What if it came in the form of an encouraging word from the girl at the local coffee shop? If so, would you notice it? Would you receive the message?

So often, even within my own personal, daily life, the voice of God came to me through other people. Often, the "angels" that I needed most came in the form of my sisters or my mother or even close friends. The term "angel," from the Greek "angelos," literally translates to "messengers." What if the voice of God came through the people you surround yourself with? Would you notice? Would you hear Him? Would you get the message?

You see, by having the much-needed shift of perspective and focus which drives the Kingdom all around you, you'll begin to recognize all the more that just as God is speaking to you, within you, He is always speaking all around you. The voice of God is never silent – especially to those who believe. As Jesus said, these signs truly will follow all those who believe – those who are able to see the realm of Heaven all around them. It's time to become more open and more receptive. It's time to begin to hear and to see the Kingdom in full operation, even within our midst!

Many perhaps find it rather shocking when I say that God also speaks through nature, as well – through the birds and through the trees. Such a statement shouldn't be considered shocking, though. After all, even Jesus himself held to this belief within his own life and ministry while here on Earth. No, it isn't some "new age" belief; it's simply the Kingdom in operation! Have you ever taken the time to notice just how often the scriptures speak of Creation – even the created things – crying out to declare the glory of God? Even within the account of Creation depicted in the Book of Genesis, we find that God created "signs" in the heavens. Even the heavens declare the glory of God and all Creation shows forth his marvelous handiwork.

"The heavens declare the glory of God; and the firmament sheweth his handywork. Day unto

day uttereth speech, and night unto night sheweth knowledge. There is no speech nor language, where their voice is not heard. Their line is gone out through all the earth, and their words to the end of the world. In them hath he set a tabernacle for the sun, Which is as a bridegroom coming out of his chamber, and rejoiceth as a strong man to run a race. His going forth is from the end of the heaven, and his circuit unto the ends of it: and there is nothing hid from the heat thereof." (Psalm 19:1-6 KJV) Yes, even nature is declaring the voice of God to humanity each and every day with every sunrise and sunset.

So often in my own life, I've found my greatest sense of peace while in nature. Often, so many of my most wonderful times in prayer and meditation have taken place while out in nature, as I've enjoyed the beauty of God's Creation. Those who know me well know that I so value my time outdoors because I know that God speaks to me even through the beauty of nature. Jesus also held to this belief. How often did he use nature to share the truth regarding the nature of Heaven? How often did he ask that those listening take time to "consider" the birds of air or even something as simple as the lilies of the field? I'm a firm believer that even Jesus realized the voice of God in nature because he realized that the essence of God is woven into the fabric of the physical, natural world.

Nothing can separate us from the voice of God! Nothing can separate us from His Presence! Not only is Creation calling out to you in an attempt to share the Kingdom of God with you, but all of life is always trying to get your attention. God is always speaking. In Paul's letter to the church at Rome, he details how marvelous and how ever-present the nature of God truly is. The voice of God is ever-expansive and all-encompassing. Marvelous things begin to happen when you live according to the Spirit!

"There is therefore now no condemnation to them which are in Christ Jesus, who walk not after the flesh, but after the Spirit. For the law of the Spirit of life in Christ Jesus hath made me free from the law of sin and death. For what the law could not do, in that it was weak through the flesh, God sending his own Son in the likeness of sinful flesh, and for sin, condemned sin in the flesh: That the righteousness of the law might be fulfilled in us, who walk not after the flesh, but after the Spirit. For they that are after the flesh do mind the things of the flesh; but they that are after the Spirit the things of the Spirit. For to be carnally minded is death; but to be spiritually minded is life and peace. Because the carnal mind is enmity against God: for it is not subject to the law of God, neither

indeed can be. So then they that are in the flesh cannot please God. But ye are not in the flesh, but in the Spirit, if so be that the Spirit of God dwell in you. Now if any man have not the Spirit of Christ, he is none of his. And if Christ be in you, the body is dead because of sin; but the Spirit is life because of righteousness. But if the Spirit of him that raised up Jesus from the dead dwell in you, he that raised up Christ from the dead shall also quicken your mortal bodies by his Spirit that dwelleth in you. Therefore, brethren, we are debtors, not to the flesh, to live after the flesh. For if ye live after the flesh, ye shall die: but if ye through the Spirit do mortify the deeds of the body, ye shall live. For as many as are led by the Spirit of God, they are the sons of God. For ye have not received the spirit of bondage again to fear; but ye have received the Spirit of adoption, whereby we cry, Abba, Father. The Spirit itself beareth witness with our spirit, that we are the children of God:

And if children, then heirs; heirs of God, and joint-heirs with Christ; if so be that we suffer with him, that we may be also glorified together. For I reckon that the sufferings of this present time are not worthy to be compared with the glory which shall be revealed in us. For the earnest expectation of the creature waiteth for the manifestation of the sons of God. For the creature was made subject to vanity, not willingly, but by reason of him who hath subjected the same in hope, Because the creature itself also shall be delivered from the bondage of corruption into the glorious liberty of the children of God. For we know that the whole creation groaneth and travaileth in pain together until now. And not only they, but ourselves also, which have the firstfruits of the Spirit, even we ourselves groan within ourselves, waiting for the adoption, to wit, the redemption of our body. For we are saved by hope: but hope that is seen is not hope: for what a man seeth, why doth he yet hope for? But if we hope for that we see not, then do we with patience wait for it. Likewise the Spirit also helpeth our infirmities: for we know not what we should pray for as we ought: but the Spirit itself maketh intercession for us with groanings which cannot be uttered. And he that searcheth the hearts knoweth what is the mind of the Spirit, because he maketh intercession for the saints according to the will of God. And we know that all things work together for good to them that love God, to them who are the called according to his purpose. For whom he did foreknow, he also did predestinate to be conformed to the image of his Son, that he might be the firstborn among many brethren. Moreover whom he did predestinate, them he also called: and whom he called, them he also justified: and whom he justified, them he also glorified. What shall we then say to these things? If God be for us, who can be against us? He that spared not his own

Son, but delivered him up for us all, how shall he not with him also freely give us all things? Who shall lay any thing to the charge of God's elect? It is God that justifieth. Who is he that condemneth? It is Christ that died, yea rather, that is risen again, who is even at the right hand of God, who also maketh intercession for us. Who shall separate us from the love of Christ? shall tribulation, or distress, or persecution, or famine, or nakedness, or peril, or sword? As it is written, For thy sake we are killed all the day long; we are accounted as sheep for the slaughter. Nay, in all these things we are more than conquerors through him that loved us. For I am persuaded, that neither death, nor life, nor angels, nor principalities, nor powers, nor things present, nor things to come, Nor height, nor depth, nor any other creature, shall be able to separate us from the love of God, which is in Christ Jesus our Lord." (Romans 8:1-39 KJV)

CHAPTER TEN

THE ABUNDANT LIFE

If you desire to hear God, then it isn't enough to love God; you must also love yourself and others. The prophetic gift, as with all gifts, operate according to love. And love, being the very identity and character of God, is the basis of even the voice of God within our lives. Not only is God calling out to you through all matters of daily life, but life, itself, is calling out to you in an attempt to get your attention. In closing, I want to share with you a very real principle concerning the truth of the abundant life. You've been given a promise of a greater, brighter future. You've been given the ability to dream dreams and to hope for a brighter tomorrow. And, as the scriptures declare, hope maketh not ashamed.

Do you truly desire to hear the voice of God more clearly and more accurately than ever before, learning to rely more heavily upon your very own prophetic gift? If so, lastly, become more determined to enjoy the journey of your life. Become more determined to enjoy each and every day as the marvelous adventure that it truly is. You've been given a gift – a very real "present" in this unique moment of time, even in the here and now. There's a lot to be said about living your life and accepting the journey of your life – especially where the Kingdom of God is concerned.

There is no "maybe" in the Kingdom of God. There are only certainties – only the sense of "knowing." The abundant life comes when you "know" that all things are being made to work together for your good and that there is no condemnation against you. You can't love your life and judge your life at the same time. Love and judgement cannot coexist; it's impossible. Something truly heavenly and extraordinary happens when you begin to love your life and when you become determined to believe in your dreams and in your God-given destiny all the more. Your perspective begins to shift from the natural to the more heavenly things and you begin to hear the voice of God all the more clearly. You become more able to recognize God in all things.

The prophetic gift operates according to love. All gifts do. When the apostle Paul, in his letter to the church at Corinth spoke of the spiritual gifts in operation, he explicitly states that the greatest of all gifts is love. God *is* love. Would it not stand to reason, then, that in order to better access God within the three-dimensional world it's important to love your life while you're here? Where there are prophecies, they will cease. Now, we know in part and we prophesy in part. But when that which is perfect will come, we will know fully. Thankfully, though, we don't have to wait for the perfection to come. When love comes and when you're able to grab hold of the revelation that you can love your life now and experience the voice of God for yourself, interacting with Heavenly realms even in the here and now, the voice of God will become merely the natural byproduct of that love. Love God. Love life. Love others. Love your journey.

"Though I speak with the tongues of men and of angels, and have not charity, I am become as sounding brass, or a tinkling cymbal. And though I have the gift of prophecy, and understand all mysteries, and all knowledge;

and though I have all faith, so that I could remove mountains, and have not charity, I am nothing. And though I bestow all my goods to feed the poor, and though I give my body to be burned, and have not charity, it profiteth me nothing. Charity suffereth long, and is kind; charity envieth not; charity vaunteth not itself, is not puffed up, Doth not behave itself unseemly, seeketh not her own, is not easily provoked, thinketh no evil; Rejoiceth not in iniquity, but rejoiceth in the truth; Beareth all things, believeth all things, hopeth all things, endureth all things. Charity never faileth: but whether there be prophecies, they shall fail; whether there be tongues, they shall cease; whether there be knowledge, it shall vanish away. For we know in part, and we prophesy in part. But when that which is perfect is come, then that which is in part shall be done away. When I was a child, I spake as a child, I understood as a child, I thought as a child: but when I became a man, I put away childish things. For now we see through a glass, darkly; but then face to face: now I know in part; but then shall I know even as also I am known. And now abideth faith, hope, charity, these three; but the greatest of these is charity." (1 Corinthians 13:1-13 KJV)

"Death and life are in the power of the tongue: and they that love it shall eat the fruit thereof." (Proverbs 18:21 KJV) Notice that the writer of the Book of Proverbs states, specifically, that those who "love it" will eat the fruits thereof. Love what? Quite simply, the life entrusted to us. When you begin to see that all of your life has been a wonderful love letter written to you by God and that all of your life has been the voice of God speaking to you, it will become difficult to not love yourself and love the journey. When you see that there were no accidences and no coincidences and that always,

at all times, you've been divinely orchestrated to experience life just as intended, it will become impossible to not love the journey you're on. When you love your journey, you begin to open your perspective all the more to the realm of God.

All of your life, even in the here and now, is the voice of God speaking to you. And so, I would ask, are you hearing Him? Most of all, are you seeing Him? Are you seeing Him in all things around you? Are you able to recognize that even in the most unlikely, most uncanny of ways the voice of God is reaching out to you to offer guidance, encouragement, and, above all, hope? When the eyes of your understanding become enlightened, as Paul states, you will move into the realm of knowing with greater confidence and with greater clarity.

ABOUT THE AUTHOR

Dr. Jeremy Lopez is Founder and President of Identity Network and Now Is Your Moment. Identity Network is one of the world's leading prophetic resource sites, offering books, teachings, and courses to a global audience. For more than thirty years, Dr. Lopez has been considered a pioneering voice within the field of the prophetic arts and his proven strategies for success coaching are now being implemented by various training institutes and faith groups throughout the world. Dr. Lopez is the author of more than thirty books, including his best-selling books The Universe is at Your Command and Creating with Your Thoughts. Throughout his career, he has spoken prophetically into the lives of heads of business as well as heads of state. He has ministered to Governor Bob Riley of the State of Alabama, Prime Minister Benjamin Netanyahu, and Shimon Peres. Dr. Lopez continues to be a highly-sought conference teacher and host, speaking on the topics of human potential, spirituality, and self-empowerment. Each year, Identity Network receives more than one millions requests from individuals throughout the world seeking his prophetic counsel and insight.

ADDITIONAL WORKS

Prophetic Transformation

The Universe is at Your Command: Vibrating the Creative Side of God

Creating With Your Thoughts

Creating Your Soul Map: Manifesting the Future you with a Vision Board

Creating Your Soul Map: A Visionary Workbook

Abandoned to Divine Destiny

The Law of Attraction: Universal Power of Spirit

Prayer: Think Without Ceasing

Warfare: Stop Attracting It!

And many, many more

204 | P a g e

Made in the USA
Monee, IL
13 November 2020